DIAMONDS IN THE DEW

An Appalachian Experience

By

Nora Stanger, M.S.

This book is a work of non-fiction. Names and places have been changed to protect the privacy of all individuals. The events and situations are true.

ISBN: 1-4107-7911-4 (e-book)
ISBN: 1-4107-7912-2 (Paperback)

Library of Congress Control Number: 2003095598

This book is printed on acid free paper.

Printed in the United States of America
Bloomington, IN

1stBooks - rev. 09/17/03

Dedication

This book is dedicated to:

My granny, Nora Maude Mitchell (1902-1979), who never turned her back on us, despite the gossip and shame. She unselfishly gave all she had to help raise us and spent her last days nurturing us.

And to my mother, Emma Jean Swango, who believes in dreaming in spite of obstacles and taught us the value of hard work and education.

Table of Contents

Acknowledgements

I was once told that we are a compilation of the people who have touched our lives, and the lessons learned from interacting with them. I have been encouraged to write a book for years by professional colleagues, friends, and family. Though it is easy for me to speak and teach, putting my thoughts on paper in detailed form has never been my strength. It is impossible for me to thank all those who have carried me through this process but there are a few who have literally held my hand as I wrote this book.

My family including my mother, five sisters and two brothers, have shared in the experiences that shaped my foundation and bolted me into the life I now live. To my sisters, Terri Baker, Ella McCown, and Linda Fraley, whom I affectionately refer to as 'the committee', you have been my champions throughout life. Thank you for insisting that I continue to share our story to encourage those still caught in the oppression of poverty. You have wisdom and strength beyond what most people can imagine. You are my inspiration. Thank you, Terri,

Ella and Linda, for editing this book, sharing your memories and believing in my abilities.

To my husband, KC, I owe more than words can express. You have supported my every dream. Your prayers have strengthened me. Your insight, advice and example have always been solid. You have given me confidence to seek and live my purpose in life. Of the many earthly blessings I have received, you are the dearest.

To my daughters, Hannah and Hope, thank you for your patience as I wrote this book. Thank you for what you teach me about life. I'm grateful and excited to be able to watch you grow! You have my heart.

Prologue

Nora Maude Mitchell was my maternal grandmother. We called her 'Granny' and a better woman could never have existed. She had no material possessions but what she had she gave unselfishly to assist my mother in raising us children. Granny was pure Appalachian. This meant she could grow an amazing vegetable garden, butcher and clean animals for meat, preserve food for winter, take care of the workhorse, make her own dress patterns from newspaper, sew our clothes, find the best blackberry patches, quilt, and make scratch biscuits like no other. She also did most of our 'doctoring' including making poultices to wrap wounds and clear chest colds and making cough syrup from Four Roses whiskey, lemon, and honey. She often sent us to the woods to pick wild herbs that she would make into medicine. I remember clearly one early summer morning walking with her past the strawberries she grew behind the smokehouse. My bare feet were soaked in the morning dew. I was moaning for something now not important. She pointed out toward the brilliant red berries that glistened in the morning sun. She said to me, "We may not have fine things like you see on TV. But we've been blessed. Look at our diamonds in the dew. You could easily walk right by and miss them…and what a treasure you'd miss if you did."

I have often thought of the wisdom in Granny's words. Now I realize that the real diamonds are the people we come in contact with each day. By not acknowledging the value of each person how many treasures have remained hidden, even to them? How many times do we miss the "diamonds in the dew?"

Chapter 1

My Story

Have you ever passed by a broken down house, windows covered by cardboard, siding falling off, trash littering the yard and porch, and a rusted out car in the yard? Have you wondered what type of people would care so little about their home? Don't they care about the environment? What are they teaching their children about responsibility and life? What type of influence will their children have on yours? Allow me to take you into my childhood home.

I was born and raised in the foothills of the Appalachians located in Lawrence County, Ohio. I was the fifth of eight children in my home. My father was in and out of our lives in my early years until right after my eighth birthday. That's when he decided to find something better for himself and left us for my mom to raise. Her one goal was to make sure we all stayed together. This was not easy for a woman with only a high school education and no work experience. Our community offered little as far as employment was concerned. Even if she had a job, what would she do for childcare?

My mother scrapped together $125 to purchase a crumbling log house up in a hollow. The house had no indoor plumbing, a coal stove in the living room for heat, and was being used as a barn when we got it. I remember the day we shoveled out the horse manure and scrubbed the floors so we could move in. We drew water from a well with a bucket and a rope, sometimes fishing dead animals out and pouring a gallon of bleach in the well to try to remedy the problem. We went to the bathroom in the woods until we finally built an outhouse across from our yard. We heated our water on top of the stove and bathed with a cloth out of a small pan of water.

The problems were only starting for my mother. My grandparents did what they could to help but were poverty stricken themselves. Also, in those days divorce was a shame to all family members and a divorced woman was the object of gossip and harassment. To add salt to the wound, my mom had to sign up for welfare. For all generations before her, no one in my family had ever had to ask outsiders for help. They prided themselves in being self-sufficient, living off the land, taking care of their own and helping their neighbors whenever they could. My mother had to face the shame of asking for help and then demonstrate her need for it. At times we would all follow behind her into the caseworker's office to prove we existed. What I noticed most during caseworker visits was that the workers appeared bothered by our needs and seldom, if ever, made eye contact. It was as though we were trying to take something from them and we didn't care about things like pride and dignity. There was always a heavy cloud over us after one of those visits.

Our lives reflected the pains of poverty. We stood in line at the city mission in the closest town for Thanksgiving and Christmas meals. We ate government commodities (powdered eggs, powdered milk, processed meat). When food stamps were created we were able to shop at grocery stores but we were constantly being scrutinized by the cashier to make sure we did not try to slip a non-food item through. We were reminded by other children that their daddies paid for our school lunches. We were not selected for school programs or activities because those making the decisions knew we could not afford the related expenses.

Through these difficult years my mother made some things very clear to her children: we all needed each other and would only survive if we were each other's champion; education was not an option but a requirement; and every person is created for a purpose—a good purpose. She suffered from depression but worked her way out of the darkness as best she could. She slept on the couch by the stove to make sure the fire did not go out at night. She read poetry to us from books borrowed from the bookmobile, taught us the constellations by laying on the grass during summer nights too hot to sleep indoors, and read daily from the red leather Bible my sisters won by selling the most garden seeds at school. My mother did not do everything right, but she did the best she could with what she had.

My family has experienced tragedies and victories, and believe it or not, I feel richer for the journey, even for the dark times. Now more than three decades later, one of Mom's children has a Bachelor's degree and five have Master's degrees. (One is working on her doctorate at this time.) Even my mother went back to school when she was 40, earned a Bachelor's degree, and taught special education for several years.

Along the way there were special people who would encourage my family. Sadly, others did just the opposite. We were bombarded with verbal and non-verbal reminders of our low status in the community and in the world. Thank goodness we did not give in to those voices. It was hard but it was not out of reach. Now I feel the need to share and encourage others who desire higher ground than they currently know. I guess the point of my story is we were valuable people even before we had college degrees and houses with bathrooms. It took a long time for us to realize this.

In this book I attempt to share my insights on life based on my experiences. There are many in the Appalachian studies field that may be offended by my frequent references to poverty within my home region. I realize all Appalachians are not poor or uneducated and I do not wish to promote a negative stereotype. Yet in reality, our poverty and illiteracy rates continue to be significant. I know the barriers that keep the Appalachians from realizing their strengths and potential. I write about these. Though I will often make statements about my culture and my people, I understand that no one can define a people with exact details and specifications. No two people fit the same mold. I do not mean to insult or assume I understand everyone's

5

experience in the Appalachian culture or within the culture of poverty. Each person has a story and the individual story is important. However, I am basing the information in this book upon my personal, educational, and professional background with the hope that you, the reader, will glean from this information inspiration to overcome whatever battles you are facing.

From time to time we all fall into some form of poverty. Whether your poverty is caused by financial, emotional, spiritual or physical reasons, no person is a stranger to heartache. I hope to continue my mom's message: We were all created for a purpose, and that purpose is good.

Chapter 2

Our Appalachian History

Our Origin

The Appalachian people have a strong and colorful heritage. Our people primarily came from the European countries of England, Scotland, Ireland, and Germany. Our ancestors were largely the peasants who were under the authority of the lord of the manor. They were yeoman farmers, having the knowledge and skills to be totally self-sufficient. They grew vegetable and flower gardens and preserved the food. They cared for and trained livestock to use as needed. They made their own fabric to make their own clothing. They knew the value of every plant and tree and used these resources for food, medicine, and lodgings. However, all their strengths could not mask their struggle. They were no more than servants to the noblemen.

They used all their skills to the benefit of the elite and were only allowed to keep enough goods to barely exist.

The dream of these strong but oppressed people was to have land of their own and to be able to take care of their families without being indebted to anyone. They did not have high aspirations of climbing the social, economic or political ladders of this world. Our people were not prone to public debate or protest. They tended to keep their ideas to themselves. Their dreams were simple and pure: "Let me take care of my own and live in peace."

When the peasants of these European countries heard of the cheap land available in the New World many sought ways to take advantage of the opportunities. Many sold themselves into indentured servitude in order to gain passage on a ship to America. They used the abundance of yeoman skills they had acquired through generations and worked out their debts. Then they moved into the Appalachian region where the availability of land allowed them to claim their dream. Some obtained as many as one hundred acres which became their cherished home.

I do not wish to ignore the plight of the Native American and the African American Appalachian heritage. Their experience has been dark and shameful in the history of the United States. Because I have limited personal experience and detailed knowledge about these valuable people in our Appalachian history I choose not to write about them. However, I want to pay respect to them and honor their strength to endure through the harshness of their historical experience, and to acknowledge the wounds we see today. I pray that people of all races, classes and experiences will receive encouragement and inspiration from the work I do.

Life in the United States

Once established on their land in Appalachia, our people thrived. They worked extremely hard to clear new ground, build their homes and barns, tend their crops and raise their families. They were often isolated from larger areas within their communities and from the outside world. They loved their families and understood their responsibilities in caring for the land that brought their survival. Perhaps it was because they had little contact with the outside world, or perhaps because their expectations for material gain and social status were not priorities. Whatever the reason, as a whole, the Appalachian people did not rise in economics as quickly as other

Americans. They were content to live the dream of their European ancestors. They had their land and could take care of their own.

Until the Industrial Revolution of the 1800s, the Appalachians did not have cash money at their disposal. When large cities opened factories and had a great need for workers, many Appalachians left their homes to obtain jobs. This was a blessing because it allowed our people to have more exposure, communication and knowledge of the rest of the world. This also had a negative impact. Families that once worked side by side everyday, and were dependent upon each other for social, emotional, physical and spiritual support were now separated from each other during most of the day. One or both parents worked long hours in the factory, while older siblings took care of the young when not in school. The family systems suffered from a drastic change of culture, and they were separated from their extended family and the mountains they loved.

During the Great Depression of the 1930s, Appalachians, like many others, lost their city jobs. However, the Appalachian still owned the family land in the mountains and returned "home" to once again take up the yeomanesque lifestyle they had known for centuries. Though times were tough for the whole nation during the Depression,

Appalachians were able to survive on their heritage of self-sufficiency. Once again, immediate and extended family members were working side-by-side for the benefit of all and the family unit regained its strength.

The coal mine industry has been a source of jobs and economic resource for Appalachia since before the 1800s. Many of our people have benefited from this industry. But in many other ways coal mining has brought a cloud over the region as dark as the dust that blows from coal burning furnaces. It was the city man who came into the region because he recognized the enormous wealth hidden deep within the majestic mountains. It was the same people who often gained access to the coal in less than credible ways. As a student at Berea College in Kentucky, I heard stories from classmates of their older relatives who had been misled by coal company representatives into signing away the mineral rights to their land. This meant the coal company had the right to strip the mountain and destroy the very land and home of the people who had trusted them, without compensation.

There was a mighty price to pay as a coal miner as well. My grandfather was a blacksmith for several mines within the Eastern Kentucky and West Virginia area. Miners had to work long, back breaking hours in deadly conditions for very little pay. At one time my grandparents lived in a company town. Their house was company owned. Grandpaw was paid with company money which could only be spent at the company store, where the prices could be inflated without accountability. I remember his recollections of 'Bloody Harlan' and John L. Lewis' fight to organize the men and demand better working conditions and other compensations for the dangerous work required of them.

With all the hardships of coal mining, at least it offered families jobs and many of our men and boys found their livelihood there. But then in the 1950s men began being replaced by machines. From the 1950s though the 1980s the need for local people to fill mining positions declined leaving the area just as poverty stricken as ever. Many of our people fled to the cities of Detroit, Pittsburgh, Dayton, Cleveland and Cincinnati to find jobs in the car or steel industries.

In the 1960s a young and wealthy politician named John F. Kennedy visited West Virginia campaigning for the presidency. He was so shocked by the degree of poverty he saw that he made a commitment to the people that if he were elected he would make changes in their economic plight. President Kennedy was assassinated before he could fulfill this commitment but Lyndon Johnson carried on his plan. The War on Poverty of the late 1960s drew attention to the economic situation of the Appalachian region. Appalachia has benefited in several ways from this crusade. The Appalachian Regional Commission was eventually established which lead to interstate road systems making accessibility into and out of the area more accommodating. Programs such as Head Start and the Bookmobile offered early and continual educational opportunities for our people.

Other efforts have not, in my opinion, had positive long lasting effects. VISTA volunteers (most often college students from outside the Appalachian region) and social agencies made the mistakes of many visiting missionaries decades before. They came into the area not understanding or appreciating the culture of our people. These well meaning people thought that they knew what was best for our people, which typically meant the Appalachian should become clones of them. They told our people that we were poor, that we should not be living the way we were, and that we were entitled to government monies to meet our needs.

Unfortunately, following the discovery of the welfare system, many Appalachians began to give up on their farming lifestyle, a lifestyle of self-sufficiency. This did not result in significantly decreasing the level of poverty of the Appalachian. Instead we now have people who for generations have become dependent upon government assistance as a way of life.

Attempts to attract more industry and employers to our region have been somewhat successful. But often these companies look outside the region to hire their management and administrative positions. Educational opportunities have greatly increased in the Appalachian region over the past twenty years. However, a significant number of our people do not take advantage of these opportunities. In spite of some improvements, Appalachians still fight negative images that are often portrayed of us.

Chapter 3

Overcoming Stereotypes

Several years ago I was asked to present a message on the importance of being proud of who you are to a large group of elementary students in a public school. Two hundred first through fourth graders sat in a semicircle on the gymnasium floor as I spoke. I began my program by holding up a picture of a beautiful, two-story brick, suburban home. This home had a manicured lawn and professional landscaping. It had a three car garage and you could see a hint of an in-ground pool in the back yard. I asked the children to imagine what type of child lived in this house. Little hands flew up to respond. I was told that the child in this house was really smart and fun to play with. This child always wore cool clothes to school. He had the neatest toys and threw the best birthday parties. He was liked by everyone at school and always made the honor roll. Everyone wanted to go to his house to play.

Then I held up a picture of a dilapidated old house. The wood siding, some of which was falling off, was bare and in desperate need of paint. Some of the windows were broken and the curtains were torn. The grass was knee high and full of weeds. The yard was covered with trash. Again I asked the young students, "What type of child do you think lives in this house?" This time hands went up just as quickly. But the description of the resident of this home was very different. This child, I was told, was mean. He bullied other children. He wore dirty, old clothing that looked ugly. He did not do well in school work and even cheated sometimes. Some children actually called this child 'stupid.' This child continually had to go to the principal's office because he did bad things. There was an overwhelming agreement that no one wanted to be this child's friend.

I then confided in the children that I am the child that grew up in the old, broken down house. You could hear the gasps of shock. I asked the students, "Do I look mean? Am I dirty? Am I stupid?" The students immediately began saying, "No, Mrs. Stanger. We didn't mean that about you." I then began my message of being proud of who you are and the importance of looking beyond the exterior to value the person within.

As I was holding up the picture of the ugly house and hearing the students' descriptions, I could not help notice a few children became very quiet and began to drop their heads. One little boy in particular actually slowly drew his legs up close to his body, then wrapped his arms around his legs and dropped his head, as in a fetal position. The shame in this child was so obvious I wanted to scream. Then when I identified myself as the child of the old house and the future accomplishments I had obtained, his head popped up, his body relaxed and he sat up tall. I could visibly watch this child find value for himself through my story.

This message knows no age barrier. When the presentation was over and I was preparing to leave the school, a young professional woman walked up to me, took my arm and quickly led me to a small room. She introduced herself as the school psychologist and began sobbing. She explained, "I am the little girl who grew up in that old house." She thanked me for my presentation and told me that my words had hit close to her experience and her emotions were overwhelming. She said, "I have fought the stereotypes of poverty my entire life. The most difficult issue I have is that deep inside I still believe that the negative labels put on me as a child are true." Stereotypes are easy to teach but extremely difficult to dispel.

Appalachians have experienced pain from the falsehood of images of our people and our culture. Many of these beliefs are based on fictional novels with characters that never existed. We have heard jokes, been bombarded with hillbilly logos, and been taunted because of the way we talk. As with all stereotypes of different cultures or ethnic groups, it is often easier to believe a characterization of a people than to get to know the people or culture personally.

Richard B. Drake, a historian from Berea College, explains in his book, *A History of Appalachia,* that often outsiders consider the Appalachian as a "peculiar people filled with superstition and infected with 'folk belief'" and "people of remarkable laziness, ignorance and violence." How do these negative stereotypes affect those of our culture? There is an ancient proverb that says, "As a man thinks in his heart, so is he" (Proverbs 23:7, King James Version). Too often in my professional and personal experiences I see the self-fulfilling prophesy of attitudes such as these. If the verbal and non-verbal messages tell a person that they will never overcome a certain hardship or that negative traits are inherently true about them, they will eventually succumb to those traits.

In addition to the battle of overcoming negative stereotypes of our culture, there is an enormous burden of shame that many within Appalachia carry. There is a secret fear that the negative attitudes about us are true and that to risk overcoming will only bring more humiliation. Those who do overcome often experience feeling as though they have to continually prove they are deserving of what they have gained. It is hard for them to relax and say, "I've done a good job." Even if their accomplishments are worthy, often the person feels as though they still owe someone. There is a continual sense that they have to keep trying to pay their debt for past poverty. But never knowing to whom the debt should be paid, they are constantly apologizing for their failures. It takes a great amount of energy and work for the Appalachian of poverty to succeed.

When I was an undergraduate student I struggled to keep my grades up the first two years. I had never been exposed to the vocabulary or the subject matter in many of my classes, plus I was adjusting to a whole new environment with an abundance of choices to be made everyday. Add to this my extreme shyness and low self-esteem. However, when I entered college I immediately declared psychology to be my major. Unfortunately, I had never had a psychology class in high school, nor had I even spoken with someone in my desired field. During my first semester I took general psychology and no matter how hard I tried, I could not score above a C on the tests. I went to the professor and shared with him the efforts I was putting into the class (studying one to two hours nightly just on this subject, going to a tutor weekly). I asked him what else I could do to increase my understanding of the material. He looked me straight in the eye and said, "Nothing. You're stupid." He then went into a ten minute tirade on how frustrated he was dealing with stupid Appalachian students and how if it were not for the research project he was working on he would leave our area immediately. (Please note: the college I was attending is known for their respect and assistance given to Appalachians. This professor's attitude did not reflect the philosophy of the institution).

Can you imagine my shame and the destruction this man's words did to my dream? I went back to my dorm room devastated. I kept the experience of this discussion to myself, too riddled with shame to share it. I questioned whether I should return home and just embrace failure as my lot in life. Despite other successes I accomplished after my meeting with him, his words would often come back to haunt me and made me more hesitant in taking risks. I am so grateful I found the strength and did not allow this insensitive man to destroy my future.

Once again I had to fight the negative stereotype of Appalachian intellect when I went to graduate school. I entered graduate school on academic probation because my graduate school entrance test (GRE) scores were below the accepted range. My grade point average from undergraduate school was good and my references were excellent. Also, days before I took the GRE we buried my granny, one of the most important people in my life. I was told by the admission committee that I would have to maintain a B average in order to be removed from probation after the first semester.

Understanding the conditions of my acceptance I boarded a Greyhound bus in Ashland, Kentucky for the thirty-six hour drive to Abilene, Texas. I had one thousand dollars (a monetary award received while a student at Berea College), one suitcase of clothes, a six-inch iron skillet, a sauce pan, a spoon, a fork, and one humongous dream to overcome the stereotypes of my heritage and become a therapist.

The first semester I took a testing and assessment class in which I learned to give individual intelligence tests. My first attempt at giving a test was observed by the professor through a two way mirror. During his evaluation of my performance he sternly told me that I would have to try harder than other students because there was one person on the admission committee who had strongly opposed my acceptance there. This was because of my 'unstable background' and my less than desirable GRE scores. I am certain that this professor believed sharing this information was going to motivate me. However, knowing that someone did not want me there was burdensome. Having to prove my value to these powerful people was intimidating, especially since I was not yet sure of my worth. I went back to my tiny apartment located in an alley near campus overwhelmed with the fear that I had failed after risking it all. Here I was fourteen hundred miles from my home and everything that was familiar. I felt very much alone.

Fortunately, within a week I gained the courage to discuss these concerns with another professor within the graduate department whom I perceived to be more accepting of me. He acknowledged the discussion of my inclusion to the program and the reasons behind the opposing committee member. Thankfully, he also explained his understanding that Appalachian students historically score lower on standardized tests. He did not view this as a sign of our deficient intellectual abilities but our lack of experience with such instruments. He encouraged me to hang on tight to my dream and to apply the energy from the passion I had toward succeeding. He stated his belief that I could succeed—and that's all I needed!

The faculty and staff of my graduate university were highly competent and professional. My experience with them was invaluable to my preparation for the profession I had chosen. They simply did not understand my culture or the enormity of the obstacles I had overcome to arrive at that point. They took a risk to accept me and I did not let them down. I was the first of my class to complete the requirements of graduation for a Master of Science degree and I did so with a 3.8 grade point average. I attribute this to my faith in God, my strong work ethic and the strength inherent in my Appalachian heritage.

Somewhere along the way people outside the Appalachian region, and to some degree the Appalachians themselves, have accepted the fallacy of a negatively skewed curve for Appalachians in the area of intelligence. Paul Slocumb, Ed.D., University of Houston stated, "Educators must be trained to focus on identifying students who have the ability to store knowledge rather than focusing on judging the merits of the knowledge the students have stored. The young student…is going to reflect a knowledge base of those things that are valued in the culture…." The normal bell curve of intelligence is just that—the norm. Some have accepted that Appalachia has a higher than normal population of people with cognitive deficits. The truth is that within Appalachia you will find the same distribution of cognitive difficulties, average intelligence and gifted individuals as with the rest of the world.

This point became clear once again when I recently had the opportunity to speak to the student body of an Appalachian high school. This school is known for their poverty and nothing positive was reported to me about the school before my visit. I arrived early and had the chance to engage one student in small talk before preparing for the presentation. This very polite young man, with wonderful conversational skills, shared with me that he was excited about the upcoming deer hunting season. I questioned him about this sport, which in Appalachia is much more than a sport. For many it is a necessary way of obtaining meat for one's family. He shared with me his knowledge of hunting, butchering his kill, and preparing the meat in several different forms (steak, jerky, sausage). I praised him for his skill and knowledge he had for this subject. A teacher nearby said, "That's nothing. You should hear what he knows about fishing." The young man beamed with pride as he went on his way. Just as he was out of ear-shot the teacher continued, "Too bad he'll never make anything of himself. He only reads at a third grade level."

I was shocked and disheartened! It was obvious to me that this young man had what it takes to 'make something' of himself. Perhaps he would never become a college professor, but I doubt his passion lies in that area anyway. This young man had the intellectual capacity to store a great deal of knowledge and to retrieve it upon demand. I am also certain that he perceived the negative beliefs around him by teachers and could easily begin to exchange this lie for the truth: that he has a purpose and that purpose is good.

Many people, despite their culture and socio-economic situation, have difficulty when first learning to read. This may be due to a learning disability, physiological reasons, lack of support at home or simply a developmental issue. In today's educational environment, professional educators and psychologists can assist many of these students in overcoming difficulties and they can become successful readers. But when the professionals are not knowledgeable or motivated in these techniques, the problem becomes the students. The students begin to see themselves as failures and as being stupid. Then the door to the dream for success begins to be shut. In effect, layers of shame begin to build within these students, paralyzing them to going beyond what they already know.

During my presentation to this high school I saw hope being inspired in the faces of the students. They obviously understood where I was coming from and knew that I wanted them to have a dream for their futures as well. Unfortunately, my concerns for these students were increased after my presentation. A woman came up to me and introduced herself as the guidance counselor. She stated, "I enjoyed your talk but it really doesn't apply to many of our students. You see, most of our students don't have what it takes to make it in higher education." I was livid! How can these 'diamonds in the dew' survive without encouragement? If those within their own culture and the mentors of their education cannot believe in them or their dreams, how will our children find the strength to take the risks demanded to achieve their goals?

Appalachians are not lazy, ignorant, or violent by nature. However, just as any other people, we can adopt these traits depending on the examples modeled for us, the opportunities afforded us, and the pressures on us. Just as others, we also have a wonderful ability to rise to greater heights when our value is validated and we are encouraged to dream.

Chapter 4

Understanding the Appalachian Student

Historically, striving for high intellectual accomplishments has not been the priority of the Appalachian people. We have struggled with regional illiteracy and truancy rates. Richard B. Drake, Berea College historian wrote, "Yet it is true that the folkish, yeomanesque Appalachian often found little of value in the "book learning" of the school, since what was emphasized at school had relatively little applicability to his real needs."

Since our ancestors first dreamed of being self-sufficient and taking care of their own, the survival of the family has been the priority of the Appalachian. Yet, where others may consider how today's actions will effect the future, often for the poverty stricken Appalachian it is the day-to-day choices that matter the most. For instance, if a single mother has a job to provide for the family and her young child gets sick, it is understood that an older sibling will skip school to care for the child. School in this situation is not the priority. Many students will quit high school if there is an opportunity to get a job, even if it only pays minimum wage. For those encouraging our students to seek higher education, this is a frustrating fact.

The Importance of Family to the Appalachian

I have often told professionals that you cannot separate the Appalachian student from his family. Especially for the poor Appalachian, who often has low self-esteem, the family is considered all they have. Even if that family is experiencing great dysfunction, the student will take extreme measures to protect and assist the family. They may fight within their own unit and even see the weaknesses within their structure, but they will form a stronghold against the rest of the world if they perceive their family is threatened.

The need of the whole family takes precedent over the need of the individual. There are often no boundaries within the family unit. To put self first is considered egotistic and uppity. For several years as a child, my family depended upon the welfare program for survival. Occasionally we kids would take odd jobs, such as working for tobacco farmers or janitor positions in the schools. It was understood that any money we earned would belong to the family unit to pay for such things as a load of coal for winter heat or to keep the electricity from being cut off. Even when family members are separated by great physical distance the needs of the family unit are priority. I remember when I was in undergraduate school my younger sisters would comb the ditches of our county road to collect pop bottles. They cashed these in at the local store in order to send me thirty-five cents in letters so I could have a can of pop when I studied. Each year at Berea I won labor awards that included a small monetary gift. Every time (except my senior award which I used for graduate school) I sent all but ten dollars of the gift back home to help the family. These acts were not considered a sacrifice or honorable. They were deeds of the heart because the family was most important in our lives.

In order to rise above the difficulties in life, the Appalachian resourcefulness and dedication to the family are strengths. When my mother went back to school to earn her Bachelor's degree, she often went to classes exhausted. At that time she was off welfare and working two jobs. We joke today about the variety of horrible cars Mom had during our childhood. Her car would often break down when she was trying to go to school. My mom was and is the most determined person I know—sometimes to her benefit, sometimes to her detriment. She would take one or more of us girls with her and we would hitch-hike the eighteen miles to town so she would not miss class. (One of the wonderful attributes of Appalachia is you know everyone in the community so we often did not have to walk far before someone would give us a ride.) Mom also had an agreement with the county sheriff that after class if we walked the two miles to his office he would drive us home while patrolling the county. I remember as a teenager being allowed by the professor to sit in the class during cold winter nights in order to stay warm. I also remember watching my mother drift off to sleep because of the exhaustion of her day. I would frantically try to take notes for her so she would not fall behind. In this manner, we assisted each other to the gain of the family.

The need of the Appalachian student to subsidize his family financially and emotionally is a great frustration to educational advisors and financial aid officials at colleges. The student often does not feel irresponsible when the summer job earnings are not available for school. Rather he would believe himself to be ruthless if he had ignored the family need and saved the money for his education.

We also share moments of trial and heartache with family members that contain emotions we cannot communicate to others. This is why just hearing the voice of a devoted family member over the phone can bring a lump to your throat after a hard day. I shared the following story at a Story Circle Workshop within the Sinclair Community College, Dayton, Ohio, REACH conference. In this session each participant was given a brief amount of time to tell his story. A topic was chosen and approximately thirty-five people, strangers until this moment, gave their stories to each other. The topic immediately spurred an intimate memory of mine as a child.

Growing up, Granny's house was located on the other side of the hill, past an abandoned strip mine. In the country, on cloudy nights, it is so dark that walking with your eyes open or closed makes no difference. At night we would walk to Granny's house by holding hands and feeling with our feet to make sure we did not fall into the ditch. Our journey meant walking down a dirt road, across the creek and out of the hollow to the main country road. Then we would walk the twisty main road in complete darkness, holding tight to each other. We would talk, laugh and often sing hymns as we traveled. I remember thinking how scary the darkness of the world around me seemed. There was such a sense of warmth in holding my sister's hand that the darkness did not render us nerveless. Eventually, we would walk around a turn in the road and see the outside light on Granny's house. I remember the sense of satisfaction I felt upon seeing Granny's light. It meant the journey was almost complete and what awaited me was the love of someone who always had room for me.

Upon remembering this story I realized the lessons I learned from those experiences. To this day I am very close to my sisters and when the dark days of life come I welcome the opportunity to hold on to those I love. I also learned that when I cannot always 'see' my way there is some Greater Source that helps guide me through the dark, twisty roads. I am grateful for the richness of lessons in the stories of my heritage.

Survivor's Guilt

A great deterrent for the student of poverty is survivor's guilt. For many, the moment the Appalachian child seriously considers separating himself from the family to go to college or the moment it dawns on them that obtaining the goals they have will make their life more prosperous than that of their family, they begin to experience survivor's guilt. There are two types of guilt or shame. The first is a healthy form of self-examination that tells us when we break our moral or legal code and demands a choice from us: 1. Confess and make restitution for the wrong done; 2. Ignore the wrong to numb ourselves from our conscious; 3. Change our moral code to fit our behavior or to justify numbing ourselves from our conscious. The second type of guilt or shame is that which is put upon us by others. We have not done anything wrong but by listening to the voices of others and our perception of what their expectations are of us, we believe ourselves to be not as good as others or, in family situations, a disappointment to others.

Survivor's guilt is a form of self-torture that distorts your perceptions of reality and inhibits your growth as a human. The student of poverty who makes choices that will eventually send his life in a different direction than that of his family often has to fight feelings of guilt that may sabotage success in his goals. Unless he is able to examine these feelings he will not be able to put them to rest.

I was recently told of a young man in West Virginia who graduated top in his class from a respected university there. He earned a degree in chemical engineering and was being courted by several pharmaceutical companies across the country. He had also been offered a position with a company within driving distance to his boyhood home. However, it only paid $40,000 a year as compared to upwards of $80,000 offered by other companies looking at him. His family and friends became livid that he would consider the other companies that would require relocation. His childhood sweetheart, whom he had always planned to marry, told him he was being selfish to consider moving. She pointed out that no one in either of their families had ever made more than $20,000 annually and they had "turned out alright." She made it plain that if he chose to take the better monetary offers their relationship was over. The guilt this man suffered in order to make his choice was tremendous and will most likely have to be re-visited time and again.

The Struggle Between Culture and Class

In his book, *A History of Appalachia*, Richard B. Drake describes two worlds of Appalachia: "the rich and the powerful, who dominate the region's life, and the bulk of the region's people, who are poor and powerless." Having grown up as one of the poor and powerless I appreciate even more the efforts of those trying to overcome poverty in the Appalachian region. Within Appalachia I see small 'kingdoms' established by those who have power. I have heard some say "I'd rather be a big fish in a small pond than a small fish in a big pond." In the 'small ponds' of Appalachia I have seen arrogant attitudes that could easily be squelched within a 'big pond' of a large metropolis. But because they do not have to hold to the accountability of a larger city they sometimes capitalize on their power. I lived in an area where my divorced mother was often sexually harassed by those in control when attempting to get what was her right as a citizen. Students whose parents are not considered valuable in the order of power often are not chosen or even considered for the benefits of social and educational activities.

Simple daily activities can bring a reminder of social standing and the response of the individual living in poverty can be easily misinterpreted by the observer. I recall that the bus ride home from school had a daily moment of great anxiety for my siblings and me. We walked out of the hollow to the bus stop every morning without much cause for worry. But on the return trip it was possible to view our barn-home from the bus for a split second as it was nestled between the hills and behind the neighbor's dairy barn. The house was detestable to look at and we were all ashamed of it. My sister, Linda, got in the habit of regularly causing a commotion at just the right moment in order to send all eyes to her and avoid the shame of our peers seeing our home. Linda risked her reputation, which quickly became that of a trouble maker, to spare us further humiliation. Rather than being a trouble maker, to us she was a hero.

Posturing is extremely important in the small pond kingdoms of Appalachia. The pecking order is well established and spirals down, with each level of power often kicking the person below them. For the person at the bottom of this order of power, the oppression can be defeating. They may feel that the odds are overwhelmingly stacked against them. This, in turn, can lead to adopting attitudes of either acceptance of a subservient life or anger and resentment that can eventually lead to violence and other antisocial behavior. Unfortunately, even some people placed into the life of those in poverty for the purpose of encouraging a better life can become the source of further dehumanization of the individual.

For my family it was the welfare caseworker who seemed to sabotage my mother's efforts to overcome poverty. I remember this woman visiting us in our home. She never showed any sign of respect or value for my mother or us children. She entered our home on visits and would abruptly check our food cabinets. If there was food in the cabinet she would demand that my mother tell her if she had worked any odd jobs to be able to afford the groceries. (Accepting even the smallest monetary gain from an odd job or even as a gift was strictly forbidden in the welfare system). On the other hand, if there was no food in the cabinet she would rant and rave about my mother not managing her food stamps correctly. This same caseworker would help herself to our garden without asking permission. I remember her taking the choicest ripe tomatoes, cucumbers and green beans in large quantities as we stood and watched. Never once did she say 'thank-you.' I guess she felt she was due this benefit since we were welfare recipients.

My mother is an intelligent woman who loves to read and learn. When my mother told the caseworker that she wanted to return to school with the hopes of getting off welfare, the caseworker laughed at her. The caseworker even threatened my mother, saying she would assure that if Mom tried to go to school she would loose everything she owned. (We think this is funny now since Mom did not own anything at the time.) In fact, after several years of welfare, my mother decided the only way to escape this lifestyle was to quit it all together and go back to school on her own accord. She worked different part time jobs and we went without medical insurance until she finished college and became a special education teacher.

There are many ways that people dependent upon the welfare system are reminded of their lack of value in society. Just recently I saw a bumper sticker on a truck that said, "WORK HARDER! There are millions of welfare recipients depending on you." I remember as a child hearing people complain when we would go to town for our monthly groceries. "I should know better than to come to town on the first of the month. That's when all the welfare trash crowd the store."

40

One young woman told me about a time when she was laid off from her job. Since she was pregnant and had another small child she signed up for the WIC (Women, Infants and Children) program through the welfare department. While she was at the community health clinic to pick up her free milk, orange juice and cheese, a woman who worked there hurried her child away from her. Busily filling out the paper work, this mother assumed the woman had taken her child to a play area. When her child was returned to her, the mother found her child had had a brief physical examination including a finger prick to determine blood type. The child was traumatized and the mother was dehumanized. Why had the workers at the clinic assumed they did not have to speak to the mother and ask her permission and presence for such an examination? Have those working within the welfare system become so calloused to the people they are suppose to serve that they no longer see their value? Do they resent those they are to serve?

It is not just the welfare workers who show resentment to those on public assistance. It is not uncommon in any office on payday to hear complaints of the high amount of money taken out for taxes. Often the focus of this resentment will turn to those on welfare.

Once a sister of mine became so frustrated with the complaints of her co-workers that she took out her check book and asked, "How much do I owe you?" Of course, her office mates were shocked. "What do you mean?" she was asked. My sister said, "I had to grow up on welfare or my siblings and I would have starved. I'm sorry that I have taken so much from you. How much do I owe you and I'll pay you back right now."

Our government has established a means to assist those of our country who are deep within the poverty level. Before a person can receive this assistance they have to prove their need. We, the American citizens, pride ourselves as being a benevolent people. We also tend to take pride in ourselves if we do not need to be a recipient of benevolence, and even look down on those who are in need. The truth is there are people who take advantage of the welfare system. And those people bring even more harsh treatment and attitudes toward those who do not cheat. Cheating is wrong and those found to be guilty of this crime should be punished. However, cheating is not just a weakness of those in poverty. I know people with doctorate level degrees making six figure incomes that cheat their employers out of thousands of dollars annually and feel justified in their actions.

Within the two worlds of Appalachia, from my experience, there seems also to be resentment when the powerless person begins to make strides to move into the powerful arena. I remember being told by a person in my childhood community that my siblings and I would never amount to anything. And then when we were one by one entering college, this same person was heard publicly complaining that the government was paying for our education and it was not 'fair.' (We did receive equal opportunity grants when going to undergraduate school). This man had complained years earlier that he had to pay for our school lunches. At the same time he did not want to see the efforts that would assure we would never have to take his tax money again.

When Acts of Kindness Hurt

Benevolence done with wrong or insensitive motivations can actually be more destructive to the self esteem of the recipients. When I was a child, our family was chosen by a women's group one year to receive Christmas presents. Initially, our family was excited about the prospects. We had known Christmas to be empty and depressing and were grateful to have something to dream about. A couple of days before the presents were to be delivered my mother received a phone call from the leader of the group. She informed Mom that they were able to purchase gifts for each child except one. This one, she explained, was considered to be too hard to buy for because of her "awkward" age. Since they had purchased several extra group-type gifts they suggested the presentless child choose from among these. The group's leader failed to inform Mom exactly which child was considered difficult. Mom told us of the problem before the gifts arrived.

I remember thinking, "I can't be the awkward child. Eleven year olds love everything. There's nothing I wouldn't want as a gift!"

Even though we wanted the Christmas presents, my family was very nervous about having guests in our home. My mother attempted to pick up the gifts from the group, but they insisted that they hand deliver our Christmas presents to us. This meant the group's representatives would travel from the nearest town down the country roads, to the dirt road filled with ruts that went up our hollow. Much to our anticipated shame, they would see our barn-home. At least, Mom thought, they would allow her to receive the gifts outside the home. However, when the women arrived they were determined on learning first hand about our living conditions so that they could report on the validity of our needs to their group.

I will never forget the four women who climbed out of the shiny, new car. They were carrying brightly colored packages, but it was not the gifts that caught our attention. The women were prim and proper, wearing wool suits, nylons and black pumps. One woman even wore a pill box hat like Jackie Kennedy made popular. Each woman's hair was perfectly done. They had rouge on their faces with lipstick that matched. They slowly looked at our surroundings in shock and horror. I am sure we were a sight. We were eight dirty, hungry children living in a house that should have been condemned. The fancy women did not attempt to converse with us. Perhaps they were too shocked to speak. Instead, they slowly turned their bodies to take in the scene. One lady had a pretty hanky and was dabbing her eyes. Then the women sat their packages on our floor and turned to leave. Once they were near their car, they hugged each other. I interpreted this as an act to comfort each other, or perhaps, they were communicating, "Job well done."

I hated those women. I hated their self-righteousness. I hated their wealth. I hated their presents because, even though we did not pay cash for them, the gifts were extremely costly to our image as worthwhile people. I have imagined many times that these women returned to their charmingly decorated homes, beautiful Christmas trees, and huge meals, and were satisfied that they had done something wonderful. Perhaps this even eased their minds about the great differences between their living conditions and ours.

A further dehumanizing aspect of this charitable act was that the women had not put names on the gifts. Instead the gifts were labeled with the sex, age and clothing size of each child. One of my sisters has indicated that if she ever writes a book about her life she will title it *Girl, 7, Size 6X.* Upon searching through the presents I discovered that I was the awkward child who was considered too difficult to buy for. I felt dejected to have been labeled this way. I chose a group-type gift, took it to my mother and asked, "Can I pretend this is for me?"

The primary mistake these well-meaning women created is an error frequently made. We must never make people our projects. People need relationships. From the relationships built we can better understand the needs and then consider how best to work with our new friends to remedy those needs. If these women had taken time to talk with my mother and get to know her heartache they would have understood her situation. Then, perhaps, they would have responded in a more respectful and constructive way. If they had come prepared to look beyond our living situation, they could have seen the hearts of the people that were housed there. If they had made eye contact and shared kind conversation, they may have seen strengths within the individuals there that would someday help them find the courage to overcome poverty. These well-meaning women could have provided more than store-bought gifts for us. Their efforts could have blossomed into a relationship and resulted in gaining additional wisdom for their lives as well.

I have found that it is often difficult for people who have never experienced poverty to understand the intensity of the psychological and spiritual oppression it brings. I get frustrated with politicians who try to prove that living on food stamps and in subsidized housing is not a difficult task. These people might even change their lifestyle and spend four to six weeks trying to prove their point. Yet the crucial difference is they know there will be a definite end to their adventure. They do not realize the sense of hopelessness and defeat that people of extended poverty wrestle with for years.

Several years ago I participated in an adult class in which the problem of poverty was being discussed. The teacher of the class made the statement that in our country there are no people going hungry or suffering due to finances beyond their control. I raised my hand and told him that there are overwhelming numbers of people within the United States who are hungry and some who are starving. I further indicated that I could take him to specific places to see this difficulty if he was willing to go. He then changed his statement to say, "Perhaps there are children going hungry because of their parent's mistakes, but due to our welfare system any hunger is due to the mishandling of funds by the recipients." This man, who had only known the lifestyle of upper socio-economic America, stated that he was convinced of his stance because he had spent a year working in a public defenders office.

I was just as dismayed by responses of the audience in the class on poverty. One class member, dressed in an expensive suit, spoke of how his father taught him to be benevolent to poor people. His father approached him when he was in middle school and asked him to name the neediest family at his school. The father took the son to the grocery store. The father-son team then drove to the poor family's house, knocked on the door and pushed the groceries into their arms. The highlight of this account was that they specifically bought each family member a toothbrush. They then made a special effort to tell the family to use the toothbrushes, since their teeth were rotting. The man in the class was proud of this experience because he now believed he knew how to treat the poor.

The teaching in this class showed me that there is a great need for a deeper understanding of the paralyzing effect long term poverty has on people. Even highly educated and experienced people can miss the point when dealing with people who are struggling with impoverishment. Though fraudulent people come in every walk of life, most people of poverty do not want a hand out. They are tired of the shame. But finding a way out of this dark pit can be overwhelming. Again, building relationships with people and encouraging them to recognize their strengths is the beginning to building self-sufficiency.

People of poverty are not to be placed on a pedestal nor are they to be trampled under our feet. None of us chose the situation we would be born into. But it is up to us to make the life we have beneficial to those we touch. The abundant life takes a lot of hard work, endurance and patience with self and with others.

It seems the dark side of human behavior knows no cultural or class boundaries. Arrogance does not equal confidence. Typically, the arrogant person is filled with insecurity. Nathaniel Branden, author and psychologist said, "There is overwhelming evidence that the higher the level of self-esteem, the more likely one will be to treat others with respect, kindness, and generosity." It is important for each of us to know we have the capability to curse or to bless others. I have found that accountability is the best way to keep our choices and behaviors in check. Choosing a life of high values, good morals and an eternal purpose is the key to being people our Appalachian ancestors would be proud to claim.

Chapter 5

The Value of Our Religious Heritage

Loyal Jones, ethnologist and religious scholar, considers the Appalachian religion to be "the key that unlocks mountain culture." He further stated, "These beliefs, and variations on them have sustained us, have given our lives meaning, and have helped us to rationalize our lack of material success. Every group of people must have meaning in their lives, have to believe in themselves. Religion helps to make this belief possible. There are few Appalachian atheists because Appalachians need God." (From *Appalachian Values* by Loyal Jones).

In the 21st Century, and especially in the world of academia, it is not politically correct to be a Christian. The Appalachian religion has been ridiculed for more than a century as being uninformed, full of superstitions and even regressive in nature. Most of the critical reports of our churches are written by outsiders, those who have no appreciation or history of the legitimate value our religion adds to our lives. Many well meaning missionaries have migrated into our mountains to enlighten us on their understanding of the true meaning of Scriptures, with hopes that this will increase our socio-economic standing. However, many missionaries have left frustrated in their efforts.

Though there are numerous major religious denominations in our region (Catholic, Methodist, Lutheran, etc), Appalachia is dotted with small independent churches. Our preachers of independent protestant churches often have not been formally educated, but have followed the "calling" of God, a very intimate experience that is life changing for the preacher and those who respect him. Many of our churches are committed to the traditions established generations before them such as foot washings, personal testimonials, and women's roles in the church. These traditions, though extremely important to church members, are often misunderstood and even ridiculed by outsiders.

Most Appalachians place high value on their belief in God, in Jesus as His Son, and on the infallibility of the Bible. Even Appalachians who do not belong to a church or attend worship regularly most often have these beliefs engrained in their consciousness. It is a part of their heritage, their culture, and their personhood. When an Appalachian student chooses to enter college, especially if they choose to leave home and live on a traditional college campus, one of the first areas of defense that they must be prepared for is the attack that will come on their religious beliefs.

When I entered college I went with the belief that God would guide me and mold me from the experiences of my life into what He purposed for me. I often met with negativism and, even at times, hostility toward Christianity in my classes. I was a shy student. I did not enter the classroom preaching or ranting and raving about Hell's damnation for all who did not accept my beliefs. Yet, when asked, I would not deny what I consider to be the foundation of my life. For this I was nicknamed 'the Christer' by one professor and frequently the target of jokes. I have heard reports from other Appalachian students who cherish their faith of being shocked and dismayed when first entering college and bombarded with the acceptable social behaviors and attitudes that are offensive to our faith. They also noted an open subsequent disrespect of their values. In an age when tolerance is the mantra of political activists, the arts and academicians, I continue to find that there is a double standard when tolerance is considered for the Appalachian Christian.

The Appalachian religion is the basis of our value system. It provides purpose and meaning in our lives. It gives security and strength during times of confusion and replenishes us when we are exhausted. My request to those in authority in universities and colleges is simply to respect the individual religious choices of your students. Don't intellectualize it. Don't analyze it. Don't ridicule it. Don't minimize it.

There is also an attempt by some to re-create the history of Appalachian religion to be more palatable to the modern view of religion in America. I recently had the opportunity to listen to a self-proclaimed Appalachian musician. He was performing at my daughter's school and I was asked to introduce him. Prior to his performance I overheard him explain his desire to share a play-party with the students. I was excited. I initially thought this would be a fun, positive activity from my culture for the students to experience.

Then I heard his "authoritative" description of this play-party. He told the school staff that this play-party was frequently used in church services. The words of the song, "We bow down to the mountain...We bring glory to the mountain..." were to be sung as the children circled in dance. When I was introduced to the musician, he commented that by my accent I was surely a real Appalachian. Then I asked if he would change the words of his play-party song to say, "We bow down to the Father...We bring glory to the Father" because I found his choice of songs to give praises and worship to the creation rather than the Creator. The man became livid! He insisted, "This is the authentic way the Appalachians of old worshiped in their churches. I would rather not sing the song than to change authenticity. If you were a true Appalachian you would appreciate this!"

In all of my accounts and experiences with play-parties, these activities were used as circle dances at community and family gatherings for their enjoyment, separate from worship. Never to my knowledge, or the knowledge of Appalachians of my research, were play-parties used in church as activities of worship. Also, while our people love and appreciate nature, never would we worship a mountain, especially in church. This man's knowledge of

Appalachian music was obviously book-learned and more a reminder of the 'Peter, Paul and Mary' style of music than Appalachian folk music. It appeared to me he had become a victim to the popular 21st Century view of religion and not of the historic religion of Appalachia. However, he is currently spreading this misinformation adamantly in his performances.

Just as the small white church buildings with cemeteries attached are scattered about our mountains, the values of the Christian religion is imprinted on our hearts. There are those intellectuals who have taken the notion that our religion has held us back. Some Appalachians adopt the fatalistic approach that "this is my lot in life, I have to accept it." But many more Appalachians see their faith and their church as the foundation of their strength. The church is embraced as a place to be trusted and continues to serve as a place of worship and community cohesion.

Chapter 6

The Dangers of Mind-Poverty

Educators across the country are focusing upon poverty as a key issue affecting student's performance. Poverty is often viewed as a lack of adequate financial resources. As a survivor of childhood poverty and a professional who battles the effects of poverty upon life success, I have noted many forms of deprivation that thwart the human spirit. A very dangerous form of poverty is that of the mind. Envy leaves us discontented and resentful. Discouragement robs us of energy and insight. Even worse, apathy blinds us to realizing needs around us. We play a comparison game, begrudging others who have more money, bigger houses, or have greater status at work or in social circles. On the other hand, to make ourselves feel better we may measure our lives against those who have less than us and become tempted to be prideful, flattering ourselves at our greater value. Poverty of the mind deprives us of seeking our purpose in life and drains our creative energy.

How do you avoid mind-poverty? First, we must realize each person was created for a good purpose. Life should be viewed as a journey to develop your strengths and character in order to become the total *you*, you were meant to be. This mindset takes away the crippling power of the obsession with financial, material or social status. Do not allow these temporary and subjective matters to gauge your value. Rather, look at specific areas of your life to see if you have grown personally. Are the majority of your efforts spent trying to look good in the eyes of others while in truth trying to hide who you are, or are you pleased with your progress of becoming the best person you can be? You must measure life by progress, not perfection or by possessions. Live confidently but not arrogantly.

The educator must encourage and even teach students to dream. I believe dreaming is the first step to setting goals. Many people come from environments where dreaming is not valued, therefore considering the 'what ifs' of life rarely occurs. A close friend who is a teacher in a very poverty stricken Appalachian area shared with me this story of his introduction to his elementary classroom. He began class one day saying, "What do you want to be when you grow up?" He went on to explain his belief that there was great potential in the classroom and tried to encourage the student to discuss the possibilities. After what seemed like several moments of silence and glazed-over-eyes from his students, one child raised his hand. He said, "Teacher, I want to draw." My friend immediately and with great excitement began explaining the wonders and benefits of being an artist. Again, he received nothing but blank stares from his students. Finally, the teacher's aide interrupted, "You don't understand. He wants to *draw*. He wants to *draw the welfare check*." What this dedicated teacher came to understand is that this student's intent was not to sponge off the tax payers' dollars, it was just that the student had never been individually encouraged and exposed to the possibilities. The students of his classroom had never learned to dream. Most were of generational poverty and the welfare system was all they knew.

Once a person recognizes he has a good purpose in life and is given permission to dream about the possibilities of the future, then goals can be set. Research has shown that people who have written goals are more likely to achieve those goals than people who do not write them down (Yale University study). I encourage people to write a life plan and break it down into five year segments. It helps to be willing to adjust your goals as you discover more specifics about it.

I often encounter people who are afraid to dream. They have had their dreams crushed by life circumstances or poor choices and are terrified to take a risk again. These same people tend to hold those closest to them back as well. Usually this is out of fear for their future, but sometimes they unconsciously or consciously think if they do not have the dream, others should not have it either. Without dreams it is hard to have goals; without goals it is hard to have direction; and without direction it is hard to have success. You have a choice in the matter. You can dwell on the past, on mistakes made or wrongs done to you. You can wallow in thoughts of what you do not have or what you have not experienced. Or, you can dream and plan for a better way. We are shaped and influenced by our past but we do not have to be dominated by it. We have to live with the past but we do not have to live as though we are still in it.

I encourage dreamers and goal planners to seek advice from those who have experience in the area of their dream. I ask them to search out people who have knowledge in their area of interest in order to gain information in advancing their goals. Whether it is a teacher, a work supervisor or a trusted counselor, allowing others to know of your goals opens doors in making your dreams become reality. It is also vital to be open to making adjustments to goals as information is collected. Unfortunately, not all people will respect the dreams. The coarseness of others must not be allowed to hinder the search for a more fulfilled life.

George Eliot, author and poet, said, "It is never too late to be what you might have been." If you are struggling with poverty it is important that you realize you are not stuck. We have the choice to move on in life and to move up to higher ground.

Finding your passion is essential to overcoming life's hardships and truly succeeding. Passion is a powerful emotion, yearning, or appetite for something. It is the longing for something better. It is a craving, a thirst, and a perceived need. Finding your purpose in life can fulfill this passion. It breeds energy and creativity. Where there is passion there is greater probability for success. A great benefit of dreaming and exploring goals is it helps you recognize where your passion lies.

Educators and professionals wanting to assist people in overcoming any form of poverty must be willing to look beyond the exterior, to the potential within the individual. This demands that the professional take a holistic approach with the student. Mahatma Gandhi, the Eastern Indian pacifist who single handedly held off war between Pakistan and India said, "In order to help the unfortunate you must become the unfortunate." The wisdom of these words acknowledges an understanding of the complexities of the individual struggle in life. The student in the classroom is often not just struggling to learn the particular academic subject being studied. There may be physical and emotional battles. The family situation may be a mess. There may be nutritional issues or sleep deprivation. The student may have financial and transportation worries. When the educator considers the whole person there may be more patience and a greater motivation to teach to the student.

We, especially within the people helping professions, must not attempt to make others into clones of ourselves. We must respect the individual differences while reflecting an attitude toward life that assists the person in bettering themselves. At the same time we must take a humble attitude asking, "What can I learn from my experiences with these whom I am trying to help? How will it make me a better person?"

I am not advocating or suggesting that the final responsibility of learning, achieving or succeeding should be anywhere but upon the individual. The educator cannot achieve for the student, but he can be a mentor, an advisor and an encourager. I remember the strength I gained each time a person crossed my path who would share, in some way, their belief in me and my dream to overcome the hardships of my past. Without those individual experiences my way would have been much more difficult and perhaps I would have given up completely. The educator will, of course, have interactions with students who do not wish to apply themselves, or who will try to manipulate to slide through with as little effort as possible. There are students who believe if they do not learn it is the teacher's fault for not teaching them well enough. Such people will usually have an empty plate. Even if someone fills it today, it will be empty again tomorrow. The problem is you do not always know who will recognize their responsibility and potential, and succeed, and who will not. Therefore, we all must treat everyone as though they are the one who will benefit from us the most.

Educators must expect results with respect. We must not 'dumb down' material for the Appalachian student. In Chapter 3 we discussed that the Appalachian is as intelligent as students from anywhere else in the world. However, many of our students are carrying baggage that can negatively effect their learning and performance. For instance, if you have a student who approaches you just before your math test and says, "I'll have to leave class ten minutes early today. I have a child custody hearing for my daughter that I have to be at immediately after class." Do you really think your student's attention and best effort will be given on your test? Would it be too much trouble for you as the instructor to say, "Why don't you come back tomorrow and take the test."?

There is a great need for those who are Appalachian and those who are attempting to assist the Appalachian to reframe negative beliefs about our people. Reframing is a technique for changing the way we think. Stress and negative beliefs are barriers to individual success. Reframing is seeing the positive side to a negative situation. There is an old saying I heard as a child, "Trouble can break you or make you." You have the choice of how to accept hardships or difficult situations. The scars of our wounds can be made into commemorations of strength. For example, as a child I often heard the gossip of the community about my family situation. Sometimes cruel statements would be said within my hearing that confined my family to a life of destitution. I remember praying daily that my life would be different than the gossip I had heard. I prayed for eyes of compassion and that I would someday make a positive difference in the lives of others who were experiencing various hardships of life. Many times difficult experiences and challenges in life can build strength of character and determination. Reframing helps manage feelings of frustration and disappointment. By viewing life's difficulties in a different manner, these difficulties can become seen as steps to success. By changing our thoughts we can change our feelings and our vision of life.

Another valuable and practical technique for success is the use of visualization. In this technique you visualize, or see yourself in your mind, actually obtaining your goals. I often use this method before I attempt tasks such as presentations, interviews or even writing this book. While I was in graduate school facing some arduous tasks, such as finishing my thesis and taking my oral exams, I would visualize myself in the specific situation I was about to undertake. I would imagine myself as calm and confident. I would smile to those in authority and see myself answering all demands of me with an assurance of success. This technique does not replace hard work, study or efforts to build relationships with those around us. But it assists in defraying insecurity and helps plant seeds of belief that you can achieve the goals of your life dreams.

The Appalachian is a person of pride who has had our dignity disrespected for too long. We do not tend to argue our point or to demand our way. You will not hear many reports on the evening news about public outcries or protests in the Appalachian area, especially rural Appalachia. We tend to keep our wounds and embarrassments to ourselves. But we also tend to have amazingly long memories. We remember who shamed us and we remember who helped us. Though there has been much attention given to Appalachian feuds (mostly fictitious), most of us would bend over backwards to avoid conflict. Perhaps these are also some reasons that risk taking for higher educational has not been a priority for us.

Chapter 7

Avoiding Money Traps

Shortly before our father deserted our family, he got a 'wild hair' to burn all of our old furniture and replace it with new. I remember the exhilaration I felt as I watched him burn our old mattresses. The new furniture was beautiful to me. It was clean and pretty, and it smelled delightfully good. I remember the pleasure of sleeping on the new beds for the first time and laying pretty doilies on the wooden end table. My memories distinctly hold the coloring and texture of the living room suite. As an eight year old girl I imagined our family having suddenly become the richest and most important people in the world.

What my child-mind did not understand was the concept of credit. Our father had purchased hundreds of dollars of furniture without actually paying for it. When he deserted us he left us a legacy of inadequacy in every sense of the word. It was not long until the creditors began calling and threatening my mother if she did not pay for the purchases. Of course, our mother had no money. I remember our family trying to avoid the collectors by hiding under the windows and beds of our barn-house as the men banged on the door. I have clear recollections of the men shouting obscenities and describing us as people who had no conscious, stealing from companies for our own pleasure. I assure you as I looked over at the faces of my baby sisters and saw the terror in their eyes, pleasure was not something we were feeling. Ultimately repossession occurred. As the men with white shirts and ties supervised the emptying of our home, they took advantage of the moment to lecture us about the foolishness of taking things you cannot pay for. The shame I felt at that moment was unbearable. I could not look at the faces of the men, but I remember their words well. The most difficult memory is of my four year old sister twirling around in a revolving chair as the commotion went on around us. Finally, one of the men stopped the chair abruptly and told her to get off. He carried the chair away while we stood watching.

Because of experiences such as these I have great empathy for those of inadequate material resources. Adults I know who grew up in poverty usually take one of two approaches to possessions. There is either fear of debt and great effort put into being frugal. Or there is the throw-caution-to-the-wind attitude in which credit card debts abound. To make matters worse there is a great amount of money spent in the advertising business geared toward tapping into our feelings of emptiness and selling the message that their product is the answer to all our fears of inadequacy.

I have a close friend who for many years was a buyer of precious gems for a major Cincinnati jeweler. She once spent a week in New York City attending a conference for the jeweler. She told me that a major portion of this conference was focused on teaching sales personnel the art of creating the "illusion of need" for perspective customers. Does that phrase slap you in the face as it does me? Our entire country has gotten too caught up in the deception that says our value is based on our possessions. Our obsession with materialistic gain has put many Americans in debt so deep they cannot imagine ever climbing out. Many unscrupulous companies actually target people of low socio-economic status for their profit. When you are poor and a company advertises the ease of renting a big screen TV for low weekly charges it's easy to think, "I can handle that."

Man vs Money

The love of money can easily take control of people and can become the downfall of character and morals. The desire for more money and possessions can jeopardize relationships and result in even the best of us showing our dark side.

Our mother would often take three or more of us girls to make a team for working in neighbors' tobacco crops. In the late fall, we would stand all day in their cold barns and strip the cured tobacco stalks, grading the leaves and tying them into large 'hands' to prepare them for market. It was cold, dirty, hard work, and we would continue for eight hours a day on weekends. On weekdays we would work after school for three or fours hours a day until the crop was completed. We were given an agreed pay of one dollar per person, per hour. We made up a great team and were known for our excellent work at a faster pace than any others in the area. I will never forget when one farmer we were working for shorted our pay by half, insisting he had already paid us the other half. My mother told him we had not received the full amount, but he refused to pay. In her mind, to fight with him over the rest of the money was too humiliating. We had already endured enough shame in being called 'welfare trash' in the community. (This same neighbor later complained about his taxes paying to keep us alive).

Unfortunately, this neighbor and his wife were also highly respected by my granny, almost as though they were the ideal married couple. After my grandpaw died Granny leased her tobacco allotment to this couple. Based on a verbal agreement, she was to receive a small fee, about fifty dollars, at the end of the season for payment. Granny felt this was a good arrangement since these were good people in her view and she could not work the fields any longer. She had made plans to use this money to buy the winter load of coal for heating her house.

During this time, a younger sister in junior-high, was active in after-school activities. The daughter of the neighbors' who leased Granny's tobacco allotment was involved in the same activities. Since we had no way of providing the transportation for this opportunity, Granny asked the neighbors if they would allow my sister to ride along with them. My sister would walk from their house to ours so that the neighbors would never be 'put out'. It was agreed upon, but my sister often felt resentment and hostility from the family as she accepted their generosity. Then late in the fall when Granny called the neighbors to ask about the allotment lease money, she was told that the money had been given to my sister. By this, they did not mean that the cash was given to her, but that they had provided this by way of giving her transportation to school events. Granny's heart was broken. She had trusted and respected this couple. She felt they had betrayed her friendship, possibly from resentment or greed. We will never forget Granny's face and voice as she learned of the neighbor's intentions during that phone conversation. Without raising her voice or making any demands, she simply stated, "If you can live with it (the money), we can live without it."

As children, experiences such as these kept my siblings and me in subservient positions. It was difficult to believe that we had any value at all. As an adult, I am now more empowered with my experiences and successes, yet it is difficult to understand the mind-set of people who would hold others back in order to feel more powerful themselves. It is nearly impossible to impress upon others strongly enough our view that people and relationships—not possessions or money— are to be considered the greatest asset you can ever have.

The Power of Money

Have you ever heard the following phrases: "Money talks" or "You can tell the men from the boys from the price of their toys?" Since the beginning of time people have compared themselves with others based on their net worth in possession-terms. The more money or 'stuff' you have is often erroneously thought to be related to your level of success as an individual. There is also the thought that the more money you have the greater degree of happiness you will experience. Instead, we often observe a rampant spending of money that does not exist through the use of credit cards and installment loans. This, in turn, leads to a downward spiraling in our peace of mind for those captured in the money trap. Eventually, we get caught up in dodging creditors, bad credit reports, and facing the embarrassment of not being able to meet our financial commitments.

On the United States currency we have a statement that most of us ignore. That motto is "In God We Trust." We carry around this statement most every day. Yet when it comes to our actions in spending, we often live as if the motto should be "In Money I Trust" or "In My Ability to Beat the Credit System I Trust."

<u>Who are the Jones'? Do we really want to be where they are?</u>

While I was volunteering at my daughter's school one day I overheard a young mother talking with another. It seemed her husband had been demoted in his job and was now making thousands of dollars less a year than before. He experienced this change because of corporate downsizing and could have easily lost his job completely. The woman was expressing great concern about keeping up their lifestyle without the additional money. She was in tears about the financial loss. What struck me most was when she shared that, though her husband had been in his new position for over three months, he had just gained the courage to tell her the night before. He was afraid to tell his wife for fear that she would be disappointed in him and perhaps even leave him over his job situation. He admitted to her that he was suffering from ulcers, insomnia, and panic attacks because of his concern for their marriage. All this was due to his fear that she would divorce him if he did not provide the lifestyle she desired.

What was most striking and tragic about this story is that the woman did not get the point! She verbally admitted that her husband had not lost his position due to his performance and that he had always put her happiness first. She spoke with great emotion as she relayed how he tearfully shared his concerns with her. She even accepted consolation from the other woman sitting with her. However, within the next few minutes the wife of the struggling man began asking those around her where she could get a good deal on a new couch! It seems she was terribly unsatisfied with the coloring of her current sofa in her den. Reportedly, the room was better suited to be decorated in spring colors and her sofa was, unfortunately, a fall color. She wondered out loud, "How can I entertain others when my colors clash so badly?" This woman did not get it! She was willing to sacrifice her *relationship* with her husband in order to have the *things* she thought would *impress others* the most.

Our marriages are not the only relationships that suffer due to unwise financial practices. We constantly model spending practices and the value we put on possessions vs relationships to our children and others who look up to us. One family I know spent thousands of dollars to purchase a new leather sofa with a built in heater and

75

vibrator. Within the first week their cat scratched a hole in the back of the sofa and the son willfully broke the vibrator. The parents decided to phone the furniture company and demand a new sofa because the one they had was "defective." What these parents actually taught their children is that it is okay to lie and to take what is not rightfully yours (steal) in order to have the best you can possibly have. Their children were heard laughing about this story later.

While speaking at a conference I was presented with this question: "I, too, grew up in extreme poverty. But now I am very comfortable financially. How do I teach my children what I have learned without them having to live with the struggles I knew?" Unfortunately, I do not know the complete answer to that question. I believe that parents must model the importance of having strong relationships with others above the pleasure of having more possessions. Too often we who grew up in poverty are consumed with making sure our children do not suffer as we did from the lack of things. We bombard them with gifts, summer passes to amusement parks, and activities that all their friends would envy. Our children may enjoy these at the moment but we are selling them a lie. The lie is that having things, going places, and being the envy of others is what makes us whole. Struggling and dealing with discomfort are usually how we learn our greatest life lessons. We should not be afraid for our children to learn the lessons of dealing with difficulties and learn to do without things or activities. In reality, if we cannot build strong relationships and fulfill a greater purpose, our lives are empty and incomplete.

How much is enough? If we equate the amount of money and possessions we have with happiness and status, it is no surprise that our lives become full of collecting (and often the subsequent tossing aside of) items and experiences that fulfill our needs temporarily. Too often this also leads to the constant exercise of paying off credit card debts and thousands of dollars of unnecessary interest payments and other related fees. In order to avoid this lifestyle we must determine for ourselves how much is enough and then make a conscious decision to live within the means we have.

Financial Planning

John (not his real name) had dreamed of going to college for years. He had solid educational goals and had taken steps since his sophomore year of high school to accomplish them. His family did not have the finances to pay his way to college. However, he was able to obtain several grants and scholarships. He also contacted the university financial aid director and was put in contact with various part-time employment opportunities on campus. John knew finances would be tight but he believed he had prepared himself well for the next few years.

What this intelligent young man had not considered was the peer pressure of students who had no financial concerns. John watched as other men in his dorm took young women out for elaborate dates. His peers also had the latest electronic devices that made life at college much easier. The straw that broke the camel's back was when John heard his friends planning a spring break trip to the Bahamas Islands. His friends told him that he deserved the trip because he worked so hard during the semester. He had felt he deserved more of their benefits for some time. They told him that he would be young only once in his life and that part of the college experience was exotic spring break trips. Unfortunately, John believed his friends.

John had been receiving credit card applications since he was a senior in high school. He told himself, "I can handle the expenses of just one great trip. I'll use my summer earnings to pay off the credit and still have money left over for fall semester." Once he had the credit card in hand, John began to frequently say, "I'll just add one more charge. It's not a large one. I can handle this. I deserve to have a little fun, too." Within a few months John had maxed out two credit cards and was thousands of dollars in debt. Discouraged, overwhelmed, and ashamed, John dropped out of school to work full time at a discount store. This story does not end here. John is currently planning on returning to college, a little later than he originally planned but as a wiser man.

What happened to John is not an uncommon story. The weakness in John's plans for life was he did not prepare for the temptations of pleasure over practicality. He did not allow himself small pleasures that were within his budget along the way. He did not take into account how his entertainment choices would effect his long range educational goals. John did not consider the rewards of delaying the gratifying experiences that are financially demanding. He also did not purposely expose himself on a regular basis with others who shared in the practice of delay of gratification.

Learning to handle finances and financial practices are just like most other behaviors. We learn from watching others. If we come from a family situation where high credit debt is common place we will most likely follow suit. Also, if we come from a family situation where lack of adequate financial resources is typical, we may be insecure about financial issues. People who are comfortable with credit debt and those who are insecure about finances are vulnerable to living a life of constant credit concerns. Credit card companies target such people and take great effort to entrap them in the cycle of high interest pay-backs.

What can you do if you know you are at high risk of financial practices? I am a strong supporter of the practice of having written goals for all areas of life, including financial. I encourage others to write lists of financial wants vs needs to help formulate financial planning. When determining your 'needs' list you must also ask yourself as honestly as possible, "Why do I need this? What will happen if I do not own this? Is there an alternative item that will serve my need just as well?" Often things that we initially believe we must have can be delayed or dismissed after honestly considering our motivation. For instance, we do not actually need new cars. A good reliable used car can meet the need for transportation and save much money to be used in other areas or saved for a future new car. If we are truly honest when making up our wants vs needs list we will find needs, while important, are less complicated that we initially thought.

Adopt a budget system for yourself. This is really not difficult to do. List your debts and your living expenses. Remember your goal is to live within your means, not to exceed it. Have a clear understanding of your expectations of your earnings. You know how much money you have to work with. When writing a budget, do not include the use of credit cards or check cashing companies as this is not solid cash and will not assist you in getting out of debt. Put your budget in written form and track your daily spending. Be sure to include an emergency fund. Also, recognize that Christmas and birthdays are not surprises. Allow a budget for gifts for such occasions. Make it a priority to stay within your budget in order that you control your finances rather than allowing your finances to control you.

One of my sisters practiced a system for years that proved very practical. After determining her wants vs needs, she named her money by writing the need on separate envelopes (groceries, mortgage, utilities, recreation, etc.). Each week she deposited the determined amount of savings into the bank, and then the budgeted amount of money for each area was put into the specific envelope. When the money in the envelop was gone, she no longer spent money for that area until the next pay period. She avoided allowing herself to borrow from one envelop to add to another. This system demanded she tighten her spending in certain areas. By using this technique and by tracking all daily spending she was able to save a great deal of money and reach her financial goals.

There are some specific practices that will help you avoid impulse or unnecessary spending. First, make a list of your financial goals and prioritize them. There is great power in written goals. Seeing your goals in written form will help you delay less important purchases in order to save for the items at the top of your list. Avoid shopping for recreation. When shopping take along a list of what you need and do not buy anything not on your list. If you find an item that intrigues you, make sure you sleep on the idea of making the purchase at least one night before buying it.

There are many resources available to assist you in financial areas. Practical information can be found in books, radio programs and the Internet. Many communities have free credit counseling services. But use caution here. Beware of companies who want to charge you a fee. Unfortunately, there are a lot of scams in the area of financial counseling services that demand a fee. There is no shame in asking for help to plan budgets and learning to live within your means. Shame will more likely come from knowing you need help but refusing to seek it out.

A Note About Completing Financial Aid Forms for Higher Education

I have frequently heard stories from guidance counselors, financial aid directors, and college access advisors of parents who refuse to complete the necessary forms for financial aid. Typically these are parents who are not college educated and/or have minimal financial resources to send their child to college. Without the completion of the appropriate forms their children have no hope of receiving loans or scholarships and will most likely not go to college. Professionals working with the student may interpret parent's reluctance or even refusal to cooperate as lack of intelligence and mean-spirited. In fact, there may be several more likely interpretations of this behavior. There could be a fear of criticism if they disclose their finances on a written form. Many of poverty live with shame because of their financial situation. The parents may be living with nightmares of past judgments from others because of their socio-economic status. They may believe that school officials and others in their community will have the opportunity to review the very personal account of their finances. (How many of us would welcome those in our community to look at our checkbooks?)

Many people have never been exposed to student financial aid forms. Aside from the personal nature of the information, the length and details of the questionnaire can be overwhelming. Parents of first generation college students may feel ashamed by their lack of understanding of the forms. It is vital that professionals encouraging the completion of such forms be sensitive to these issues of judgment and misunderstanding. The parents must feel valued and respected in order to feel safe in sharing their financial information in student financial aid forms.

·

Chapter 8

Keeping the Appalachian Student in College

When a student from a minority culture takes the step to go to college, there are often greater pressures and obstacles to overcome in order to complete the goal than for students from other situations. This is especially true for students who have no history of family attending higher education. The experiences he confronts and the relationships he encounters during the first semester and the first year are critical to his success.

I left home for college at the age of 17. I had always known I would go to college and even where I would go. Berea College in Berea, Kentucky is a unique school that serves primarily Appalachian students. This college has a wonderful work-study program to assist students in their financial needs. It also has high academic standards.

For me it was the one way out of poverty and I had longed to attend since I was ten years old.

I was not the typical American college student. In my mind there was the constant reminder of the poverty I had left behind. I knew I would surely return to it if I failed. I was not a strong student academically. Due to extreme stress within our family structure, I had struggled with my grades throughout my high school years. I had never made it into the honor society and the guidance counselor would not have selected me the "most likely to succeed." Yet, I had the dream to overcome the hardships I had known and felt I had to try.

When I arrived at Berea, I marveled at the luxuries provided for me. I had a twin size bed all to myself. (As one of eight children in my home, we slept two or three to a double bed). I had my own desk, chair, dresser and closet space. There were indoor bathrooms. I did not have to wash my hair by having my sister pump water straight from the well over my head. There were washers and dryers available and I did not have to carry any water from a well. When I did my laundry my hands never stung from the cold and never became red or sore from getting chapped. I had clothes that were considered "mine." Always before my sisters and I would share every article of clothing and would even discuss at the beginning of the school week who would get to wear which jeans on each day.

What I treasured most about those first days at Berea College was the food in the school cafeteria. I was allowed to go to the cafeteria three times a day and eat all I could possibly want. I never had to worry about there being enough food to satisfy me or that they might run out. This was also the same everyday, not just at the beginning of the month. (People who have had to survive on food stamps will understand this dilemma. By the end of the third week of the month we would be out of food and would begin scrounging for it. I remember when one sister and I were shaking from lack of food. We secretly found a large onion, cut it in half and spread mustard over it. We greedily ate it and then felt guilty for not sharing it with the others. Today my siblings and I can still remember becoming so excited on the night before the first day of the month that we could not sleep. We knew the welfare check would arrive the next day and we would have food.) But at college there was such a variety of food choices that it was almost overwhelming at first. Believe it or not, I actually lost weight my first semester because the whole experience was too good to be true and I often could not eat.

The hardest part of my initial days at Berea was the pain I felt when other students did not realize that we were surrounded by abundance. I found myself frustrated by what the others were not seeing. I also remember feeling overwhelmed with guilt. (See the Survivor's Guilt section of Chapter 4) I felt guilty because I knew my family back home was not enjoying what I had available every day. I missed my family terribly but I had no desire to return to the darkness of my home. That, too, made me feel guilty. I was consumed with fear that I would fail at what I considered as my only chance to leave poverty. If I had to return home, how would I face my community, many of whom expected me to fail? I was a fearful, lonely young woman, socially backward and fighting for my life in a way, it seemed, no one even imagined.

Now as I look back on those days, I have a sense of relief and satisfaction. I have succeeded in completing my educational goals. I have dealt with the contradicting emotions that had at one time exhausted me. However, even now I have times I need to re-visit and attend to those emotions. Yet, I truly believe that the hardships I experienced, once hated and had worked so hard to be free of, have helped me become a more complete person today.

We are all important, no matter what difficulties we have to endure. We all have a good purpose in life, no matter what our current status or what the community may think about us. We all need encouragement to ignite the process of becoming who we are meant to be. It is my hope that my efforts will offer comfort and encouragement to others who strive for higher ground.

My initial experience with college is not unique to me. I understand from consulting with several colleges and universities within the Appalachian region that there is typically a mass exodus of freshmen students within the first five weeks of their arrival on campus. Often this is because the students and staff are not prepared for the culture shock that occurs when a student is immersed into the college lifestyle. Many of these students are living in dorms that can hold more people than there are living in their entire home community.

During the orientation ceremonies of my first week in college, a presenter stated that we as freshmen were getting ready to embark on an adventure that would change us forever. He said even if we left college and went home that day we would no longer be the same people as we were when we left our family. I am sure the speaker meant his words to inspire and excite us. I, however, was terrified by the thoughts that entered my mind. I loved my family intensely and I loved the image of what type of person I wanted to be. I was frightened that somehow these changes would take the essence of who I was away from me. What I did not understand at that moment and what I believe now is one constant factor in life: THINGS CHANGE! The key in dealing positively with change is in knowing the choices we have and being prepared for the changes that are bound to happen. Most of the time, we have the option of being in control of the changes in our lives. Too often we allow others to control the options for us. This is why it is critical to know what our alternatives are. In this manner, we can learn to embrace positive changes in our lives and thrive as we live our life goals.

Educators, advisors and mentors can greatly assist the Appalachian student by sharing their personal successes and failures. Too often we who have 'made it' in our careers demonstrate a form of false advertising. We stand before the student poised, confident, often well dressed and manicured. They see us driving fancy cars and living in nice houses. They can easily think that we could never understand what they are going through. After all, we appear to have it so easy. I remember coming out of a professional meeting once and having a friend say to me, "If I didn't know better I'd swear you were one of those rich, well-bred, women by the way you carry yourself." I did not want to take away from her apparent attempt to compliment me but I was thinking, "I am well-bred, and you can ask my Granny about that!" Perhaps, we need to share our struggles with our students more and admit we do not have it all together.

While I am not advocating telling our students every intimate detail of our struggles or mistakes, I think it is vital that they know we had to sacrifice and work terribly hard to get where we are. All of us have had a point in time (or many times) when we wondered if we would ultimately succeed or fail. All of us know failure. All of us have had sleepless nights of worrying about decisions made or that need to be made. It is important for our students to realize that if we can know success, they can know it as well. They must know that they are not alone in their doubts and fears, but that these can be overcome.

It is also beneficial for students to have someone they can talk with about their fears and failures. Many times in a new experience a student is embarrassed to ask questions, and may not even know what questions to ask or where to go for help. It is well known in the field of psychology, when under extreme stresses or during times of exhaustion, people often fall back to the coping mechanisms they learned as children. If the student in question came from extreme poverty where education was not valued or if they were from a dysfunctional environment, this student may understandably return to coping mechanisms that could sabotage their educational or professional goals. Once such a student fails, they most often will not try again due to the shame experienced and the fear of future failures. College students are often assigned an advisor when they enter school. However, these advisors may simply sign off in approving class schedules and have no personal contact with the student. Consequently, not all advisors should be personal advisors. Having a life coach to discuss the struggles and reinforce the accomplishments of the student in his experiences can be an encouragement and may mean the difference in failing and succeeding. A life coach who understands the sensitivities of their situations could also be available for students in reviewing and discussing personal and educational goals, social issues, family issues and other areas that may be a concern. Never underestimate the power of encouragement that can come from one who has been there!

Chapter 9

Preparing the Appalachian Student for the Real World

Have you ever had the desire of longing for a better place and then working toward this dream for an extended length of time, only to discover the 'dream' was not exactly what you had expected? There are many of us who encourage students to go for their dreams and cheer them on from the sidelines as they strive through the emotionally exhausting mood changes and the sleepless nights of completing assignments. Unfortunately, we do not often prepare the students for the realities of life after they have obtained the college degree. Once the Appalachian student of poverty successfully achieves years of educational demands there is often an emotional let-down. This is especially true of the student who is the first of their family to go to college. Such a student may have spent years of effort, frequently putting his pride on the line, to succeed in overcoming the barriers to higher education. They have braved the challenges of breaking the cycle of poverty, and risked the criticism of family, community, faculty and peers. Once the goal of obtaining the degree is met, we cannot assume the student is prepared for what happens next.

I was ill prepared for the requirements necessary to complete my professional and educational goals. I did not know until my junior year of college that I could not reach my professional goals with merely a Bachelors degree in psychology. When I realized I would have to go to graduate school I was overwhelmed emotionally because I had no family connections with someone who had gone beyond an undergraduate degree. I was confused by the choices before me and very fearful of the thought of taking out student loans to finance this new goal. Because of the poverty I had known as a child I was terrified of beginning my adult life by going thousands of dollars into debt. And yet, in order to become what I had always dreamed of becoming this was the challenge I would have to confront and surpass. Had it not been for the friendship of my dorm parents at Berea College, I might not have continued my education. Dan and Joy

Lucas took me under their wing and did a lot of hand-holding as they walked me through the graduate school admission process. Dan and Joy both have their doctorate degrees and they encouraged me by sharing their experiences. They told me that they believed in my abilities. They helped me complete forms, encouraged me to go to a university that would be a good fit for me, not only educationally, but emotionally and spiritually as well. They wrote letters of recommendation on my behalf, drove me to the GRE exam and helped me plan for the experience of moving to another area of the United States. Mentors, such as Dan and Joy, are a God-send in preparing a student embarking on new experiences.

Seeking the Dream Job

One of the greatest misconceptions that first generation college graduates have is that having the degree guarantees them the dream job. They have been encouraged to go to college because a college degree is essential for a better life. Often the student then believes that having the degree assures them of prosperity. Unfortunately, the truth is that having a college degree simply allows them to compete with the rest of the world of college graduates. In reality, gaining their first employment in the area of their degree is largely dependent upon the economy in their geographical area, the availability of employment positions, and their interview skills.

There are steps students can take prior to completing their degree that will assist them in gaining employment after graduation. They can research job possibilities represented in the area of their degrees. Students can seek out job opportunities in those areas and try to gain work experience either part-time or during the summers until their degree is completed. In this way the student will be able to build a resume that will be attractive to future employers. These experiences will be helpful in determining which type of work environment fit the student's interests and strengths.

An important consideration for the new college graduate is the interview process. From developing a resume and cover letter, to speaking on the phone with the secretary of a potential employer, it is critical that new graduates know how to communicate the impression they want to make. First impressions may be the only ones we get to make.

The job-seeking student should be versed in interview skills. Simple facts such as arriving a few minutes early for the interview, choosing appropriate clothing for the interview, being courteous and using the appropriate vocabulary are essential. It is important not to wear strong cologne or perfume. Also, bold or heavy make-up is not typically appropriate for an interview. Making eye contact and smiling warmly makes the interviewee appear more approachable. However, laughing or giggling at inappropriate times can be a turn off to an employer. Prior to the interview the prospective employee should make a list of questions to ask the interviewer about the job and should take the questions on a pad of paper to the appointment. Notes may also be taken on this paper during the interview. Many employers like seeing this type of interest in a potential employee. Though salary is important, it should not be the topic of initial questions. It is important for the interviewee to remember the interviewer's name as well as the name of the secretary. Saying goodbye to both of them, calling them by name before leaving is a courteous touch. (Everyone likes to know their name is remembered). Once home, the job-seeker should write down the highlights of the interview. Questions should be listed that were spurred by the interview discussion. Also, the job-seeker should make a list of pros and cons to getting this job. This information should be retained to use if a second interview with the same company is granted. Following up the interview with a letter thanking the interviewer for the time and consideration, as well as noting specifics of the interview conversation shows interest in the position.

It is critical for job-seekers to realize, that even after gaining an employment position, they will continue to make an important impression throughout the first several months of a new job. If this is a salary position and not hourly, it is helpful to make a point of arriving to work a half hour early and leaving a half hour late each day during the first six months. This indicates to supervisors that you are committed and dedicated to being successful in your work. Avoid absentees at work unless absolutely necessary. Try not to get caught up in office gossip and do not overextend coffee breaks. When you agree to accept an employment position you make certain unspoken promises. Being true to the work ethic and values for which you want to be remembered are essential.

Often students are disillusioned with their first employment position. The student must understand that most often they will begin their work experience in an entry level position, even with a college degree. However, having the degree will make it possible to earn promotions and work toward more responsibility in their career. This is why it is important to research the company and the position in question prior to and during the interview process, to understand what will be expected of you, and what opportunities will be afforded to you.

High priority should be given to avoiding job-hopping. It is not unusual for the new college graduate to have two or three jobs before he finds his niche. However, leaving a series of jobs after just a few months can be alarming to future employers. Many young professionals have a misperception that they should enjoy every aspect of their employment position. The truth is there are many details to even the best job that are mundane and anything but gratifying. Unless you face moral, ethical, or legal issues that are unacceptable, once you commit to an employer you should honor that commitment.

Education does not end with obtaining the college degree. Many careers require obtaining continuing educational units in order to retain certifications or licensure. This must be expected and respected. Professional employment, and life in general, should be viewed as an extension of the classroom. All of our experiences, even negative ones, form who we are and should help build the person we wish to become.

Coping with Family Expectations

While the following issues of coping with family expectations are not experienced by all Appalachian families, they are not uncommon especially for families where generational poverty has been the rule. Therefore it is helpful for the student to consider and be prepared for such trying times.

As previously stated, the family unit, rather than individual needs, is often the most important element to the Appalachian student. Because there may be few boundaries in these family units, the successes of the student can affect the entire family. The pressure on the student to prove himself is great, especially in the family where no one has ever gained a college degree. The same parent who may have proudly slapped the back of the student on graduation day and said, "That's my boy" may as easily demean him when he does not get the first job for which he interviews. If the degree does not land a job for the student soon after graduation, it is not unusual for him to hear statements such as, "You thought you were so high and mighty, didn't you. Well, you're no better than the rest of us. Come on College Boy, show us how smart you are now." Not all families will respond this way, but it is important for the student to consider and be prepared for such possibilities before they occur.

Once the student has a job it is also not unusual to find the family planning how they want to spend the money earned. Remember, the student may have spent their entire childhood turning over money earned from odd jobs to the family. After beginning a professional career they may have the experience of visiting home and learning that a family member "borrowed" their check book to go to the local general store for a few things. Or the new professional may arrive home, notice his truck is missing and find out later that a family member needed the truck for something and simply entered his house and took the keys.

Establishing healthy boundaries within the family unit is often the most critical and sensitive of all efforts the student has to accomplish. The intensity of love the student has for their family and the devotion they feel toward them is not in question. It is important to understand these family members are not consciously attempting to take advantage of the student. They simply have a need and they do not see a distinction of "mine vs yours." In such a family what belongs to one, belongs to all. However, as the student takes steps to become established with dreams of their own family, the family of origin may feel rejected and judged.

An outsider might look at this family and determine them to be dysfunctional. Yet, it is imperative to consider that most dysfunctional behavior may at one time have been very functional. In fact, the behavior may have been necessary for the survival of the family. What makes this behavior dysfunctional is that, as the family situation changed and these behaviors were no longer necessary, the behaviors did not change as well.

Learning when to say "no" to family members is one of the most difficult lessons the student will have to learn. The truth is whether considering family members, employers, co-workers or friends, we teach people how to treat us. We should not complain that no one respects or appreciates us if we have never made it known how we expect to be treated. This means establishing healthy boundaries and sticking with them. There are risks in taking such a stand.

Boundaries are borders or limits that are communicated to others to indicate what behavior is acceptable and what is not acceptable. It is well known that situations and relationships that have clear boundaries tend to be more secure because all parties involved know what is expected and how to proceed with the relationships. There is typically more respect for individuals in relationships that have clear boundaries. For instance, out of respect for my sisters' time, I need to ask before planning to spend the weekend with them. If I have a need that I think they might be able to assist me with, I will ask for their help rather than expect it or insist on it. If they state that they cannot meet my need, I must accept their decision with respect and not take their response as rejection. In an employer-employee relationship, I know what time I am expected to be at work, what duties I am expected to perform, and what my financial compensation will be for my efforts. Setting boundaries with family members, especially when no boundaries have been established before, is very sensitive and can become emotionally volatile at times. Anytime the functioning of a relationship is being questioned or is in the process of being reestablished, individuals within the relationship will feel vulnerable. This can lead to heated discussions. However, boundaries can be established successfully, in a healthy manner so that all persons can benefit and have stronger bonds as a result.

Code-Switching

Upon leaving my childhood home, I spent four years in the Appalachian region on a traditional college campus and then moved to west Texas to live in an apartment for two years while completing my graduate degree. I married a city boy from a suburb of Detroit and we eventually settled in the greater Cincinnati area. I established a successful career in the field of psychology. During this journey I have built strong relationships with professionals and individuals from nearly every walk, culture, class and religion. Fortunately, I have earned the respect and affection of many of these people. My life today is a world away from the life I knew when I lived in the hollow of my childhood. However, that does not diminish my esteem for my people or my heritage.

Whenever people leave a minority culture to establish themselves within the majority culture they often have to give up something of themselves to be considered successful within their new environment. During this exchange there are times that the individual feels they no longer fit in either world. It is important for the Appalachian student to be aware that they will need to consciously determine what their core value system is, what they are willing to compromise, and what they will not give in to. If the student leaves their childhood region they will have to learn how to function socially and emotionally within the new environment. This is true even if the student is merely moving from a country home to a city within the Appalachian region.

Code switching is the process of choosing how you will respond to a situation which is different than your culture of origin. Code switching is important to consider because without understanding the choices to be made, the person from the minority culture can feel a type of code-schizophrenia. One may wonder, "Who am I?" "Am I pretending or faking for these people?" "Do I fit anywhere?" When the Appalachian student establishes ahead of time what core values to live by, the student then feels more at peace when confronting new cultural experiences. For instance, I have determined that who I am in any situation must not violate my religious beliefs or my heritage of a strong work ethic and loyalty. If the situation does not offend these issues then I can adjust to whatever is at hand. I will not, however, deny or change who I am to please the situation.

Taking this stance does not prevent the cognitive dissonance that often occurs for the people from a minority culture trying to balance the world of their origin and the world of the majority culture. Not long ago I visited the poorest school in Ohio. I presented my motivational program and saw the hunger for a better life in the eyes of my high school audience. Afterwards, I mingled with the students. I heard individual stories of poverty and a great desire to know a better life. The oppression of their situations was unmistakable. One young man explained that he had been in a very difficult home of violence, substance abuse, and lack of adequate resources until he was able to move in with his aunt. "How is it now?" I asked. He proudly pulled on his shirt and said, "Now it's great. I get to go to Wal-Mart just about every month for some new clothes." Another young man said, "I know what you're talking about when you described the broken down house you grew up in. At my house I don't have to look outside to see if it's raining. I just walk in our kitchen. There are huge holes in the roof and the rain pours in." In my presentation to this group I mentioned that my father had deserted our family. A freshman boy took me aside and said with shame, "My parents are divorced. My daddy did something very bad." I told this child that I was sorry he had experienced this, but then I continued, "You do know, don't you, that you don't have to make the same choices your daddy did, you get to choose the type of man you want to be." I watched this child's face brighten and his response was a surprised, "Yea, You're right!" I left the school feeling I had just stepped back into time and had experienced my own childhood through these students.

Two days later I was at a luncheon with friends of mine. These are wonderful women with hearts that are generous and kind. However, I was struck with the topics of conversation. They included whose child was performing a viola concerto at her school that day, the color scheme of the décor of someone's den, and the gourmet cooking class one was taking. These women had no idea of the life the children I had just visited with were living. I found myself torn by the two worlds I was experiencing. Both worlds have people of great value but they struggle with very different issues. I excused myself early from the luncheon, emotionally exhausted. I took a couple of days to reevaluate my approaches to these different worlds.

Considerations of Spoken and Unspoken Rules of Culture and Class

There are many ways Appalachian students are asked to change who they are to satisfy outside cultures. One of the most common and immediate changes requested is in the way we talk. I am saddened when transplanted Appalachians tell me they were instructed to change the way they talk or else face rejection by employers, co-workers, and friends. I knew one man for several years before I discovered he was originally from deep within Appalachia. This man is a highly successful businessman who talks like the man on the national evening news. His mannerisms and lifestyle speak nothing of his heritage. When I asked him about this his response was, "In order to be successful I had to shed every trace of Appalachia. Otherwise, I would never be where I am today." (I personally have to ask, "Where are you today if you have totally denied the origin that shaped you?") A young Appalachian woman, who moved far from her home region, shared the reaction of her employer when he first met her. He said to her, "The first thing we are going to do is to teach you how to talk!" He and others then made the removal of her accent their project. Another woman was met by her university professor when she started college and was told, "If you are to be successful you must learn how to talk without that accent." The professor was from the Appalachian culture and was teaching at an Appalachian university. In all three of these examples, the people gave into the pressure to consciously change the way they talked in order to be more like the majority culture, and in effect, began their journey to stop identifying with the culture of their origin.

I am well aware that when we leave a geographical area we can lose our accents merely by lack of exposure. That is understandable. However, when we accept the encouragement or consciously choose to change the way we talk for the specific purpose of hiding where we are from, we unconsciously accept the shame that others have placed on our people. I believe that many Appalachian students need to expand their vocabulary and that proper grammar is necessary for good communication. Often this comes simply through educational experiences and exposure. But to deny our accent or certain phrases we share with our people is unnecessary for personal and professional success.

Most forms of cultural differences are more subtle than language differences and more difficult to prepare for. For example, when I was a student at Berea College most students were from similar backgrounds. Everyone wore blue jeans to class and very few students had cars. If they had a car it was a used car, or at least modest. When I got off the Greyhound bus in Abilene, Texas to begin my graduate school career, I was overwhelmed by the cultural differences. Many of the students were from wealthy families. Some women dressed in designer clothes as though they had just stepped out of a fashion magazine. I saw real gold jewelry and diamonds on students. There were expensive sports cars driven by undergraduate students. Being a part of a social club was a priority for many of the students. There were gala affairs that required formal attire. My experience of extreme poverty made adjustment to this new environment difficult.

Early one morning I was walking across campus and came upon a Porsche parked by a dorm. As a college prank someone had covered the luxury car with Oreo cookies, not one inch of the car was untouched. Though some student(s) saw this as a fun joke, I stood in the parking lot and cried because the world I was in at the time had no awareness of the economic nightmare many in my home area were experiencing. I did not feel equipped to communicate this need and frustration to those in my new home. The priorities these students had were light-years away from the priorities I had.

There are unspoken rules lived by in each social class. The concept of "entertaining" was something I discovered much later. In the middle and upper-class world entertaining seems to be very important. Having friends and co-workers into your home for dinner is something that is often planned for in great detail. Much attention is put into decorating your house in just a certain way and the dinner table does not just hold the plates of food; it has to be attractive. I remember going to the bridal registry with my future mother-in-law. She explained what gifts I should register for, pointing out that guests want to know the specific item you would like to have. (I felt embarrassed even registering, as though I was begging for gifts, and assuming something I should not.) I looked at the price of every item and chose the least expensive of what was offered. I was then taken to the dinnerware section of the store and told to choose a pattern of dishes for both fine china and every day use. I could not believe that not only were you expected to ask for dishes but asking for two different types was considered normal.

Within different cultures there are social evaluations of individuals as well. A few years ago, I was invited to attend a house warming of an acquaintance. She had just moved into an amazing house and wanted to share it with her friends. As I mingled among her guests, I stood near a circle of women who were talking. After a few moments one woman said to me, "What neighborhood do you live in?" When I told her she literally turned her back on me and resumed her conversation as though I was not there. Unfortunately, even though she knew nothing about me, she and her friends determined that since I did not live in an impressive enough neighborhood, I was not worthy of their conversation.

On the other hand, if these same women visited my home area they would be scorned or laughed at for their arrogance. As my granny always said, "We put our pants on the same way, one leg at a time." When a transplanted Appalachian is placed in these different social and cultural circumstances they have to determine if their need for inclusion is greater than the value they have for their heritage.

The people who work hard to gain acceptance from the majority culture often lose respect from their friends and family in their minority culture home. They may be perceived as uppity and 'above their raisin.' The transplanted Appalachian may then be caught between two worlds and left to wonder where they belong. We are not damaged goods to the rest of the world! When we, the transplanted Appalachian, determine to be proud of our heritage and recognize ourselves to be valuable people, we communicate this security to those of different cultures. We then are able to find people who are very much like us even though they are of different backgrounds. We can all learn to delight in the differences among ourselves and others. We can establish ourselves within our new world as successful and still be genuine to self and others.

Survivor's Guilt Revisited

In Chapter 4, I wrote about the impact of survivor's guilt on the student who makes choices that may make their lives more prosperous than that of their families. I feel the need to restate here that such issues of guilt for the student, because of their success, may have to be addressed from time-to-time throughout their lives. The best way I have found to deal with these emotions is to keep the lines of communication open with those who are most important to us. We must do whatever we can to live in peace with all people, especially within our family. We need to continually encourage them to know their value, to seek their purpose, and to fulfill their dreams. Yet, we should not feel the need to sacrifice our good purpose in life in order that others do not feel uncomfortable with our successes.

Chapter 10

Revisiting Our Heritage:

On Whose Shoulders Do We Stand?

In our fast paced world of constant change it is easy to become detached, even indifferent to our ancestors who worked and sacrificed to realize their dreams for the future. Perhaps their purpose was to pave the way for us. However, in Appalachia, I fear, we have allowed the "progress" of life to cloud our minds to the deeper meaning of our ancestors' efforts. Their faith in God, belief in family, work ethic, respect, and appreciation of the gifts of creation have somehow lost significance to many of us. We have tolerated the stereotypes others have laid upon us and allowed these to permeate our images of ourselves. We have never been stupid or an ignorant people. The laziness that might be seen in some of our people is often a response of feeling overwhelmed by the darkness and depression of poverty. Yes, there are those in the culture of Appalachia who tend toward violence. This is a trait that knows no cultural barriers. Violence that is not for self-defense or in the defense of those we love is often born of abuse, discouragement, pain, or intense frustration. I do not condone this violence, but I understand it.

There is great value in embracing the strengths of our ancestors. Knowing the wisdom and tenacity of our people reminds us of how we can persevere against great odds. We have a strong heritage and this, I believe, is passed through the generations if we choose to take hold of it.

My granny, Nora Maude Turner Mitchell, was born in 1902 to a farming family in Lewisburg, West Virginia. She only had an eighth grade education, but became certified by the state to teach in a one-room school. She married when she was nineteen years of age and then turned her focus toward her family. She and my grandfather had four children. Granny was also a self-taught mid-wife and delivered many babies in her community. Her own twins (one of which was my mother) were born at home prematurely. One baby was estimated to weigh less than two pounds and the other baby was less than three pounds. I remember Granny saying the babies were scary to look at and their sculls were like the soft membranes that cover eggs before the shell is formed. Three days later when a doctor came, he told her these babies were not meant for this world. He instructed her to set the babies aside and to wait for their death. What the doctor did not know was that life was extremely precious to this Appalachian woman and she was determined that her babies would live. With the help of her mother-in-law, Granny made a bed for the babies in the seat of a rocking chair and lined it with lamb's wool. She constantly kept the babies rocking in that chair-bed. Granny also kept a fire burning in the fire place and would heat towels that were used to wrap the babies in to keep them warm. She fed them with an eye-dropper. Not only did both babies live, they were of normal development and normal to high intellectual ability.

Today with our modern medical technology we understand that premature babies need constant motion which helps their circulation. Also, such babies have difficulty holding their heat. Therefore, they are placed under special heat lamps in order to keep them warm. How did my granny, with no formal education, know these things in 1932?

Granny knew which herbs to pick in the hills to make medicine. Today we recognize that 85% of all medicinal plants that grow in North America can be found in the Appalachian area. Not many Appalachians know which plants are medicinal and how to use them in beneficial ways today. For that matter, how many Appalachians today can make poultices or cough syrups that are effective against infections?

My grandpaw, George Dempse Mitchell, was born in 1893 in Tazewell, Virginia. Grandpaw had less education than Granny. He was a blacksmith and worked for coal mines companies throughout the West Virginia and Eastern Kentucky region. This man could make fine precision tools by striking metal against metal, as well as by the sound, look, and feel of the finished product. He trained his own work horse and could control the horse in the field by simply yelling out "gees" and "haws". Grandpaw made his own horse shoes and then shod his horse. He knew how to find veins of coal close to the surface of the mountain and would drill out just what he needed for his family. He knew carpentry skills, lumbering skills, and how to make charcoal. Grandpaw raised vegetable gardens, hay, and burley tobacco without the use of modern machinery. He could hunt and skin a wild animal and prepare it for Granny to cook.

Today it takes computer generated machines to do the blacksmith work that my grandfather did by art and instinct. People in this day and age would not have the strength or knowledge to run a farm without electricity and gas powered vehicles. The simple tools Grandpaw used to make the sled drawn by the horse in the field are considered rustic and out dated. But he functioned well with them and was able to care for his family. In many ways life today is easier because of our modern conveniences; but then again, we have lost much if we cannot appreciate the work of our ancestors.

There are countless Nora and Dempse Mitchell's in the history of Appalachia. It benefits us to re-consider the memories of our people who have gone in generations past. They tell us of the faith, strength, and character of the Appalachian. This is the faith and strength that sustains us today and will carry us into tomorrow.

It has been said that we are surrounded by a great cloud of witnesses. I cannot help but wonder if included in that cloud of witnesses are the ancestors that prayed, nurtured, worked, dreamed, and believed before us. I imagine my grandparents, their grandparents, and their grandparents before them standing in Heaven cheering for me, especially in my darkest days. This thought is both comforting and motivating.

What does it mean to be Appalachian? On whose shoulders do we stand? We carry the legacy of those who have gone before. Theirs was not a legacy of material possessions, educational degrees, or accolades. They have given us faith, a strong sense of family, encouragement to continue, and a desire to thrive onward. We must remember this legacy. We must not allow others to define who we are.

My name is Nora Lynn Swango Stanger. I am intelligent. I am committed to my God. I work hard. I am sensitive and generous to the needs of others. I love my family deeply. I know heartache and depression. I rejoice in good times and in friendships. I can meet the challenges of life. I have discovered and am living the purpose of my life. I have strength and experiences yet to be tapped. I am Appalachian, a 'diamond in the dew.'

Sources

Parts of this book originally appeared as articles written by this author in *The Appalachian Connection,* a newspaper published out of Cincinnati, Ohio during 2002. Along with my personal experiences and discussions with family members I have gleaned from the following sources for the contents of this book.

Chapter 2: Our Appalachian History

Richard B. Drake, *A History of Appalachia.* Lexington, Kentucky. The University Press of Kentucky, 2001.

Chapter 3: Overcoming Stereotypes

Richard B. Drake, *A History of Appalachia.* Lexington, Kentucky. The University Press of Kentucky, 2001.

Paul Slocumb, "Giftedness in Poverty." *The Gifted Education Communicator*, Winter 2001, vol 3, no. 4.

Chapter 4: Understanding the Appalachian Student

Richard B. Drake, *A History of Appalachia.* Lexington, Kentucky. The University Press of Kentucky, 2001.

Chapter 5: The Value of Our Religious Heritage

Loyal Jones, *Appalachian Values.* Ashland, Kentucky. The Jesse Stuart Foundation, 1994.

About the Author:

A child of poverty, Nora Stanger grew up in the foothills of Appalachia. Nora is a 1980 graduate of Berea College in Berea, Kentucky with a Bachelor of Arts degree in psychology. She continued her psychology studies in Abilene, Texas and earned a Master of Science degree from Abilene Christian University in 1982. Her professional experiences include providing psychological services to people with disabilities, consulting school systems on the Appalachian culture, and motivational speaking. In 2002, Nora established Higher Ground, an effort to encourage children and adults of poverty to finish high school, plan for and attend higher education, and expand their personal vision to a greater level than ever before realized.

LaVergne, TN USA
02 September 2009
156678LV00004B/29/A